Melissa Hill was educated at Sarah Lawrence College in New York where she studied economics. In 1994 she joined the Equity Research Department at the merchant bank JP Morgan Securities. After getting engaged to her husband in 1997, she moved to SBC Warburg in London as a European Equities Analyst. She is now a housewife. Melissa lives in Kent with her husband Lance, two children and Chester the dog.

THE SMART WOMAN'S GUIDE TO STAYING AT HOME

How to walk away from the working world and keep your independence

Melissa Hill

3 5 7 9 10 8 6 4

First published in the United Kingdom in 2001 by Vermilion
an imprint of Ebury Press
Random House, 20 Vauxhall Bridge Road, London SW1V 2SA

Random House Australia (Pty) Limited
20 Alfred Street, Milsons Point, Sydney, New South Wales 2061, Australia

Random House New Zealand Limited
18 Poland Road, Glenfield, Auckland 10, New Zealand

Random House South Africa (Pty) Limited
Endulini, 5A Jubilee Road, Parktown 2193, South Africa

The Random House Group Limited Reg. No. 954009

A CIP catalogue record for this book is available from the British Library

ISBN 0 09 185596 9

Printed and bound in Great Britain by
Mackays of Chatham, Ltd.

To Shannon and Cindy,
my favourite housewives

Contents

Acknowledgements

The *Smart Woman's Guide* could never have been written without the help of many people. Thank you to Babyworld and ECO Parent Link for their gracious support and to the wonderful women at iVillage.com for all their laughter and brilliant ideas. I am also indebted to the women from Parents Place who politely read all my early drafts with such patience and still said it was good.

I am deeply grateful to my agent, Mary Bruton, for being in equal parts cheerleader and taskmaster. Thanks are also due to M, for her generous efforts in making sure I didn't get carried away, and to Mandy Kingsmill for putting the commas in the right places. I owe a great deal as well to the grandmothers and Karen Ferris for keeping the girls and the dog out of my office.

Finally, I give all my love and thanks to my daughters, without whom I could not be a mother, and to my husband, without whom I would not have had the chance to be a housewife.

Introduction

Generations of women have fought for equal access to the opportunities on offer to men. However, at the beginning of the twenty-first century, women in their child-bearing years are still dropping out of the workforce and no one really seems to know why – no sociologist or government focus group, anyway.

Feminists have long trumpeted work as being the route to real fulfilment, but unfortunately for many women work can actually be miserable, stressful, exhausting and sometimes totally dehumanising. The money just does not make up for the grief. On bad days at the bank where I used to work a colleague would usually ask why we were in this business.

'I'm in it for the glory,' I retorted. 'Why are you here?'

Other women really do enjoy their careers, but find the strain on their families or their conscience too much to bear. They are leaving work to find a better life.

However, leaving work does not mean that all your problems will disappear. *Redbook* magazine and Women.com surveyed working and at-home mothers in the United States and found that either situation can be equally unfulfilling or unsatisfactory. From both groups of women, 15 per cent reported feeling depressed, angry or hopeless, while just over 30 per cent said they felt 'successful'. Roughly 40 per cent of both groups reported feeling 'frustrated'.

There are hundreds of factors that go into making your life, both at work and home, happy or not. However, if you choose to be at home full time and have the loving support of your husband, you will have a greater ability to enjoy your time away from work. Whether or not you take advantage of the opportunity is entirely up to you.

I cannot give you a list of things to do, as if there is some formula for the perfect life. What *The Smart Woman's Guide* can help you do is manage the many problems that housewives have in common and reveal to you some of the hidden opportunities that lie at home, unseen by those who have to work full time. If you decide to leave your job, this book can help you build a foundation for uncovering the miraculous life you could be living in just a few months from now.

1
And. . . what do *you* do?

When my baby was about three months old we returned to England from an extended stay in the United States. Only a few months before I had left my career which had taken me from Wall Street to the City, both places where titles sometimes seemed more important than talent. On the plane I filled in my immigration card without a thought, until I got to the 'occupation' box.

I used to be able to write all sorts of impressive job titles, but this time I was stumped. For a laugh, and to see if immigration officers actually read the cards, I wrote 'Domestic Manager'. I thought that sounded more senior than 'Domestic Engineer'.

Going through immigration, I handed the officer my card and passport. He asked the usual questions, glanced at the card and said, 'Hmm, don't you mean housewife?'

I laughed. Deep down, though, my soul shouted, 'I am smart! I can do maths in my head that would make you dizzy! I've met important, powerful people who consulted me for advice! I am no mere housebound drudge!'

However, no matter what I wrote in that precious little box, the fact remained that I was indeed a housewife. I could dress it up whichever way I liked, but people wouldn't look at me any differently if I announced that I was a Domestic Engineer or anything else. Why did I want to impress an immigration officer? I will never see this man again in my life. While he has the power to stop me entering the country, would my title help sway his decision? What about the checkout lady at the bookshop? How about the young man who sold me my last car?

None of these people give one jot about who I am or what I do. They certainly wouldn't respond to the news of my domestic situation with 'Oops! Sorry Mrs Hill, we don't sell cars to housewives.' They gave me no respect when I was an investment banker, and it bothered me because I had invested every bit of my being into getting that title.

There is more power in calling a spade a spade than in trying to sell it as a 'definitive botanical engineering implement'. The fact of the matter is a housewife is a housewife, and it is a fabulous job. Today when asked about what I do, I am pleased to say I stay at home.

Some women may find this book threatening, a throwback to the bad old days when men kept women from pursuing their dreams. They fear a return to women seeking the path of least resistance, when women were expected to stay at home and be grateful. However, as men become more accepting of women's freedom to choose their own course, women are now the oppressors, asking every woman to sacrifice her values on the altar of feminism. Quaking with fear at the horrors that lie in a life at home, we comply, and work and work and work.

How has this happened? Why are women determined to work and frightened to stay at home? Why should the very idea of becoming a housewife leave us shaking like Scooby Doo in the old coal mine?

Presumably you are reading this book because you are thinking of giving up your career, but the decision leaves you in a cold sweat. You do not have to have a super-powerful position to feel that you are giving up a valuable part of yourself by leaving work. Even the lowest paid positions held by women are invested with pride and personal sacrifice. What a job symbolises to a woman is the same, whether she works on a factory line or runs a multi-billion-pound corporation. Giving up a role that has brought so much independence, even social status, is very stressful.

Some women don't have the luxury of choice and have been forced out of work through redundancy or illness. If you are at home as a result of circumstances beyond your control, you are probably beyond stress, maybe even living in a state of terror. There is nothing worse than feeling out of control, especially because today it is commonly accepted that we can control our destiny through sheer will power and intelligence.

Deciding to leave work without recognising your fears can make the transition from work to home difficult, if not completely impossible. Fear is a crippling disease. It often lies at the root of other, more superficial negative emotions. Cruelty, suspicion, envy and anger frequently arise out of a base of fear. We have all seen ourselves act out these emotions against ourselves or our loved ones, and have resolved to do better in future. However, without recognising our fear, our efforts to be more patient, trusting and kind will be thwarted. Call me crazy, but I suspect that is the kind of Mum you want to be, so we have a little self-analysis to do.

Women in your situation are generally facing a number of worries all at once. It is hard to make sense of all these feelings when you are caught up in the middle of them.

The easiest fears to talk about relate to the outward trappings, and how society will react to you giving up work. These are fears of losing prestige or respect, facing financial hardship, and a feeling that your education and career will have been wasted if you leave now.

What these worries have in common is the emotion of pride. Somehow, you may believe that without respect, money and a consistent track record of success you will not be able to hold your head up. You worry that you will have nothing left to show for your life. No one will be proud of you any more; you will not be proud of yourself. The question 'And what do you do?' raises the horrific scenario that all that you could reply in honesty is 'Nothing'. These worries are easy to rationalise, but unless you know better it is easy on bad days to believe that without work you are indeed nothing.

From here we move to the very real fear that only work can provide deep emotional satisfaction. After all, you have been a great worker, but you have no evidence that you will be a good full-time mother. In fact, you may worry about being a 'Bad', 'Angry' or 'Boring Mum'. On top of this is the fear that leaving work will mean social isolation, leading to boredom and ultimately, depression. There are plenty of mothers at home who are stuck in this cycle, but with a little advance planning on your part and some loving kindness from your husband, it doesn't have to be this way.

You can take control of all of these fears. You cannot change society, but you do not have to take social standards so seriously that they discourage you from looking after yourself and your family in the manner you want. You control your own feelings and, if you think that you want to be at home, all these worries can be dispelled with the proper mindset.

Respect

> 'I feared the most that I would be known as no one but Mummy and not as a person anymore.'
>
> *Cristi, housewife of three years*

The practice of respecting people has eroded over the past century, and I don't mean just in terms of manners. An attitude that respect must be earned has crept into the fabric of society as the strict divisions in class structure have dissolved. I am certainly not calling for old social habits to be restored. All that bowing and scraping before your betters is not at all desirable. However, feminism, and indeed any good fight for equality, has called for respect to be paid according to the quality of the person and their work, rather than according to gender, colour or social status. Lacking any trappings of 'good work', however, individuals may wonder if they deserve respect.

Money seems the quickest way to gain respect. Those who can toss money about, showing tangible proof of what good work they must obviously perform, assume that they have earned everyone's respect. In order to have money, you have to work, and off you go on the treadmill that has been wearing you down.

Where does this leave the woman who labours long hours solely for the benefit of her immediate family, and earns nothing?

I attended a university with a primarily female student body. The general atmosphere of the school was of course feminist and politically to the left. One day in my economics class, the conversation turned to stay-at-home wives. The general consensus was that these women had a very poor life, and the young women in my class were glad that their futures did not hold such a dreadful fate. I never thought I would myself eventually become a housewife, but I did not necessarily agree with the rest of the class. I worked at that time in a shop between seminars, and saw women who stayed at home with small children. They seemed to be having a pretty good time. How could I pity women who were so content?

Ah-ha! My bright young colleagues had the answer. Women at home were just ignorant. Just as Lenin realised with his Communist revolution, if people do not know they are oppressed, they think they are fulfilled. Or they voluntarily give up the fight and, because they have no self-respect, convince themselves they are better playing the passive, submissive role.

If you grew up surrounded by women with this sort of attitude – that housewives are ignorant while the enlightened, the strong and the good go to work – no wonder you fear leaving the career track. Who wants to be seen by their peers as ignorant? Who will respect someone who apparently has no respect for her own talents?

Former career women who trumpet in the press that 'being a parent is the most challenging job I've ever had' don't help matters much. There are not many people who think mothers sit around eating chocolates and dusting their tiaras. We working women, too, are wise to words like 'challenge', which really mean hard work and late nights cleaning up someone else's, well, you know what I mean. In fact, plenty of working women do not feel particularly respected at all. So if having a successful career does not produce respect, where does it come from?

The way you are treated by others is directly linked to how you feel about yourself, and the way you behave will affect whether you are respected or not. If you respect yourself, you carry yourself differently, and others will automatically admire your style, your confidence, your *je ne sais quoi*.

Think back to times in your life when people and events just arranged themselves perfectly. I can remember a party I went to once. I was not wearing anything unusual, just my favourite dress and shoes I had owned for years. Work had been going well. I was single and just enjoying myself. That night, my friend, a stunning blonde with almond-shaped eyes and a captivating Russian accent which normally made men weak at the knees, pulled me aside to ask what was going on.

'What do you mean?' I laughed.

'Everywhere you go, men are turning their heads to look at you. Whatever you've got, I want some!'

I certainly wasn't dressed to attract attention. My favourite dress was hardly even fashionable, with a high neck and an ankle-skimming hem. The only thing I had that night was clarity. I knew what I wanted from my job and my social life. Knowing where I was going in life meant I could relax about all the niggly things – money, bills, boys – that might pop up today. Most of all, I had respect for every aspect of my life. The high points of my life, as I look back, always coincided with a decision to appreciate my circumstances as they stood at that moment, while picking very clearly a course for the future. Self-respect, then, does not stem from what you do as a job description, but whether you honestly feel you are living a good and noble life *right now*.

Respect from others is also bred by your treatment of others. If you do not feel properly respected, you may stamp around trying to terrorise people into thinking you are important. Or you may wither and try to be obsequious, maybe hoping to convince someone to give you a break in life. People are not stupid, though. Gruff behaviour doesn't usually win you any respect and weakness is usually seen as an invitation for people to wipe their boots on you.

A perfect test for respectful behaviour you can use on yourself is to think about how you treat waiters. I don't know what it is about the food-service industry, but some people feel that waiters are the modern day version of servants who should patiently bear all kinds of abuse and silly, lord-of-the-manor behaviour.

I first noticed this relationship between waiters and customers when I was young and my parents took me to dinner at sushi bars. Sushi chefs are respected as artists in Japan, but they are also expected to be sympathetic listeners and entertaining conversationalists. My parents made sure I understood that the chef was a man to treat with honour and great courtesy. So, nothing was guaranteed to ruin an evening at the sushi bar like a bolshy, drunk patron who insisted on using the chef or the environment as the butt of his jokes.

On the flip side are the people who are ever so grateful a waiter has even paid attention to them. It is not luck that gets you service in a restaurant. It's a combination of expecting reasonable service and trusting the waiter to be a professional.

Do you demand that waiters patiently stand around while you decide what to eat? Do you try to engage them in pointless conversation with the goal of making them look foolish in front of your friends? Do you use them as straight men to your jokes? The next time you go out to eat, even if it is just for a pizza, observe how others relate to the staff. You'll learn some amazing things about respect.

Another test for respectful behaviour is to watch how people treat children, not only their own children, but the children of others. When I was growing up, I was fortunate enough to meet a few adults who were actually interested in talking to me. They didn't ask me if I liked school, or some other boring question. They would ask something very interesting. For example, was there really a drug problem in schools like the newspapers all said? Who would I pick in the elections if I could vote? Did I think children should have jobs after school? In other words, they spoke to me as if I were an adult. You don't ask other adults you barely know if they like their jobs or their bosses. Why ask it of a child?

Somehow, this idea that children have interesting things to say has stuck with me and I love talking to children now. Sadly, I see parents all the time who do not show the least bit of interest in understanding how their child is experiencing life. Completely normal behaviour for a certain age is just met with impatience, while signs of precociousness receive only amused smiles.

The lesson children learn from this kind of treatment is that you exert power by being rude and directing your attention selectively. When the children grow up, they'll believe that the person with power can be rude to people of no consequence, like children and waiters. Teaching children manners is not easy, but treating children with indifference, impatience and condescension when you are in public teaches them nothing.

Think back to situations in restaurants, or involving children, and how they relate to people you have respected in your life. You may find that the people you admire most treat waiters and children with enviable graciousness. Respect and wealth, you see, are unrelated. You do not need an amazing career to gain people's respect. You merely need to have respect for yourself and for others.

> 'My fear of just being known as Mummy has come true, but that's okay . . . Being at home with my kids is the best thing I have ever done.' *Cristi*

Managing with less money

> 'I worried most about coping on one wage with an extra mouth to feed.' *M, home for five years*

What about the financial side? Can you afford to live on only one salary? I have a few theories about the economics of being a housewife:

Housewives cost less than career wives

If you have children and give up work, of course you save on childcare, which can cost anywhere from £400 to well over £3,000 per month. Many women suspect that their pay cheques fund the nursery! Where is the reward for working in this situation? If you're not convinced you want to be at work, you are not fully enjoying the experience and are giving away your money at the same time.

Childcare is in fact a major drain on a family's second income. Kelly, who lives in Lincolnshire, found the burden insurmountable. 'I wasn't well with morning sickness before my eldest was born so I gave up work when I was three months pregnant. Then, after [my son] was born I couldn't get anyone to look after him without paying more than I earned.'

The more money you earn, the more you will spend on finding the best care for your children. If you are heavily pregnant with your first child while reading this book, you have probably already weighed up all your childcare options. If you haven't, you are in for a treat-and-a-half.

Many families know from experience that in selecting care you will get what you pay for. Generally an au pair is not going to be as skilled or dedicated as a trained nanny. A babysitter is not going to be as reliable or as sophisticated as the staff at a day-care centre. If you are a working parent, you probably know that as soon as your annual pay rise comes in, the search for better childcare will follow.

The rudest surprise of all when it comes to arranging care is that the consistency is generally poor no matter how much you spend. A nanny is probably the most expensive care option, but many families find that they are lucky to keep a nanny for more than a year.

Turnover in nurseries is much higher, and I have heard nursery nightmare stories that would make your hair curl. Meanwhile, no one can love your children as much as you unless it is Grandma, who would hack off her leg with a butter knife to keep her grandchildren safe. However, many women moved away from their home town to get their great careers and are now too far away for Grandma to help out full time.

I do not want to slander the dedicated people in the childcare industry, however these professionals are grossly underpaid given the demand that exists for good care. Combine poor pay with stress and abuse by employers and I would be job-hopping too.

I don't need to tell you about a mother's guilt and childcare. You are probably already an expert in the guilt department. Suffice it to say, your salary will probably never cover childcare that can compete with your own loving attention. So, if you are unhappy about it, why pay for it?

There are many other costs that disappear once you stay at home. Over a month, halve the gourmet coffees purchased every morning because you needed a quick break from work and you have already saved your family over £60. If you bought lunch every day, there is another £60 a month, at least. You have just paid for one week's groceries (or even two weeks' if you are on a tight budget) right there. Include the cost of commuting, dry cleaning, clothing expenditure, and the tights you ladder practically every day, and you may find yourself saving an additional £200 a month, if not more.

Writer Christine Davidson, in her book *Staying Home Instead*, reckoned when she was working full time that, after deducting her expenses, she only contributed about £30 a month to the family income. So much work, guilt and stress and the family was only better off by the amount of money her daughter could earn babysitting for a few days a month. They decided it was not worth it, and Davidson resigned from her job. Making a few changes in lifestyle, such as going to the cinema once a month instead of twice, had them instantly living within one income.

This is not unusual. Another mother I know who was made redundant said, 'When we started looking at the figures, we realised it was borderline whether it was worth me working. Then we looked at the pros and cons to each member of the family of me working and money was the only reason to work. As I would not have contributed much, the other factors outweighed it.' This process of assessing the cost of working clinched the decision for her to stay at home.

Take some time to write down your work-related expenses. You might find, as some women have, that they are actually contributing little to, if not draining, the family finances by working full time. Furthermore, since a housewife's job is to look after repairs and even manage the finances, you may find you spend a little more time searching for bargains, getting good quotes for repairs or building work, even paying the bills on time for a change. All of these savings amount to real money in your pocket.

Taking good care of a house can pay off, too. We recently sold our house and made a profit of over 120 per cent. In that one transaction I, the housewife, made more money than most people earn in three or four years – and that is money that goes right to the bank, tax free, not some theoretical value of cooking and cleaning. As a working woman I would never have been able to interview five estate agents, negotiate down fees, handle the visits from surveyors and other troublemakers, quiz viewers on what they thought of the house, ensure the house was spotless and smelled nice at a moment's notice, and keep the front path swept and the front door scrubbed. One viewer, who had visited several houses, commented that 'It is so lovely to see a living kitchen!' Does your home radiate life, or chaos and neglect? More importantly, is your property making money for you?

You can get everything you need, if not everything you want, on one salary

Advertisers would have you believe you need all kinds of stuff. You do not. Your kids do not need every new toy or pair of trainers they see, and you don't need better clothes, a more powerful car, exotic holidays, or even a bigger house. Not being surrounded by work colleagues, you may find there is less peer pressure to 'keep up', and this alone will save you more money than you can imagine.

Competing with the Joneses is financially destructive. The best cure for this damaging mindset is a reality check. When we were a two-income family, we still felt financially stretched. We were spending nearly every penny that came in, if not more, every month. When we began looking at how we would pay for daycare while I continued my career, we had to take a long look at our spending habits.

There are thousands of families who survive, not in the lap of luxury, but not in the throws of bankruptcy either, on one salary. The trick is not to buy lots of stuff while on one income, but to have a good life without spending lots of money. There is no point in looking as if you are one of the top ten or one hundred richest families in the country when you are already financially okay. If you do not feel well off, then you need to get a grip on your spending habits.

Let me share a dirty little secret with you about rich people. They are cheap. They cut those pot-scrubbing pads in half so that they will last longer. They are physically incapable of throwing a paperclip away. When they do not like a service charge or an interest rate, they ask to speak to the manager to suggest that they will take their business elsewhere. Rich people jump on freebies like bloodthirsty lions. They furnish their homes in antiques because they cost less than new furniture and they just might increase in value. Think about it, isn't 'antique' just a fancy word meaning 'used'?

They avoid debt like the plague. It is true. A rich person will buy a three-month-old used car with cash and ask for an alarm system to be installed for free. They would rather be run over by a combine harvester than buy a new car on credit. I have read countless articles about successful heads of industry who shun the rule 'To be successful, you must project an image of success'. Over and over you read about multi-millionaires who drive five-year-old Volvo estates because they can safely put their dogs in the back, and anyway the insurance is lower. So start thinking humble, not flash. Demand more for your money and your expenses should be down in no time.

Besides, most of the best things in life are free. Husbands' top vote for their favourite no-cost pastime goes to sex, but there are many other things you can do together without paying a penny. Since I left the workforce my husband and I have rediscovered card and board games, have more energy to debate what we hear in the news, and luxuriate in whole weekends working in the garden. We can then admire our work with cocktails in hand at sunset and over coffee every morning before my husband leaves to catch his train.

Cheap hobbies can be very fulfilling. My husband loves to do gardening and landscaping himself. One spring, he insisted on seeding quite a large patch of lawn rather than laying turf. Not only did we save money, time and effort in seeding the grass, you should have seen how excited he was when the first baby shoots came up. He dragged me out of bed to make sure I admired them properly.

Another couple I know go swimming during the week. An annual family pass to the swimming baths near us costs just £25. That is less than one family visit to the cinema, and is probably 30,000 times more fun.

After years of crashing out in front of the television at the end of a 12-hour workday, finding these activities required deliberate thought on our parts. When we first stopped watching television, my husband would ask every night 'What shall we do?'

'We could talk.'

Shock would cross my husband's face. 'To each other?'

When thinking about how to cut the family expenses, consider hobbies carefully. If riding horses is a passion for you or one of your children, think long and hard about whether it is a luxury. If a husband has been playing golf every Saturday since he was ten years old, asking him to resign from the local club may hurt the family, even if it allows you to balance your budget. True passions are not luxuries. They are an expression of one's personality, and a reflection of what is good. Never discourage talent. Find other ways to cut your expenses.

When I began my life at home, I became very interested in computers and the internet. Needless to say, our phone bill gave my husband palpitations. It was difficult to go on-line during off-peak times because my freedom was dictated by the baby's schedule, and in the evenings I wanted to be with my husband. After many months of discussing and sometimes arguing about my passion, he began to see that my interest in the internet meant that I had given up some of my other, vastly more expensive, pastimes of hanging around auctions and going shopping. My new interest had connected me with new friends, and I became involved in some very interesting projects.

As the novelty wore off, the phone bill reduced slightly, but my projects became ever more fascinating. Today, I teach older people about computers and set them up with free e-mail accounts so that they can communicate with their far-flung families. I offer these classes for free because my love for this technology is so great. Also, spreading my social network in the community in such a positive and fun way is worth much more than money.

Passions, you see, do not have to be addictions, sapping attention and money away from the family. Your passion can add tremendous value not only to your life, but to the life of your community. Don't ever discount a hobby as unnecessary. They are, indeed, vital to living a good life. Try looking to save, instead, on what many people call 'essentials' such as food, clothing, housing and toys. It is easy to lose sight of what really is essential.

Food

At the supermarket, because we have to buy so many items, we can easily lose track of what we are spending. The clue that you are wasting money is in your fridge. How much food do you end up throwing away? How many tins are piled in your larder that have been there, uneaten, for over two months? I know how it got there, of course. You bought in bulk because of a special offer. Well, storage space costs money in the form of the mortgage you took out on your house or in the level of rent you pay. Throwing away food because it goes bad is just throwing money in the bin. Supermarket specials are not always a good way to save money on food. The way you pick up these special offers is by browsing.

One tactic to control supermarket browsing is to use the handheld scanners available at some supermarkets. One housewife I know is on a very strict budget. She scans each item and once the total hits £50, she pushes her trolley to the checkout. She knows what she really needs and she has to fit it into a fixed amount of money. This is smart shopping.

Having your groceries delivered can actually help you save money as well. We have started buying our groceries on the internet. I have found that, because I am not picking up items absent from my list, our grocery bill has been cut in half, even with the delivery charge on top. Like the handheld scanner, the internet service keeps a running total of how much you have spent. If you do need to stick to a budget, it is much easier to tick items off a list if you have spent too much than physically walk something back to its shelf. A typical shopping 'trip' on the internet takes about 15 minutes, compared with between one-and-a-half to two hours spent driving and shopping. We live a long way away from the closest supermarket, so the £5 service charge actually makes up for the petrol I would have used driving to the shop.

Review the food you have hoarded in your cupboards, vow not to cook more food than your family will actually eat, then come up with a shopping list that actually meets your family's nutritional needs for the week. Buying more than you need just to be on the safe side is really just money wasted.

Clothing

A large financial drain for many families is clothing. Young children don't need brand-name, or even brand-new clothing. This is not an opinion. It is a fact. I decided soon after my daughter was born that she didn't need to wear newly-purchased pyjamas as I am the only one who ever sees them. I have since graduated to enthusiastically accepting hand-me-downs and frequently dash into charity shops for a two-minute flick through the children's rack.

If you want your children to look especially presentable in public, iron their clothes. Well-pressed clothing is miles more impressive than fresh-from-the-shop new outfits. Colour co-ordination also makes a strong impression. I use dungarees and pinafores in very neutral colours to be the main items in my children's wardrobe, while making sure tops and socks can mix and match. This builds a large number of outfits, with a limited number of pieces of clothing.

Buying for future children, if this is a possibility for you, will save in the long run as well. If you are about to have a baby girl, allow yourself to buy only a few pink things. Aside from that, go for gender-neutral colours. That way with future children you won't have to buy a completely new wardrobe.

If you are reading this book eight months' pregnant with your first child, be aware that babies grow very fast. Everyone has been telling you how babies grow quickly, so you have probably stopped paying attention. This is how fast babies grow: you could be buying complete wardrobes every four weeks if you insist on buying only baby clothes that fit at the time of purchase. This is expensive.

Let relatives spend money on those cute super-tiny babygrows, because your baby will probably only be in them for about three weeks. This is true. You will barely be able to walk, but you will have to go out and buy an entire set of bigger clothes for this kid. The alternative is to send your husband shopping for baby clothes, and you don't want that to happen. So, any baby clothes you buy, buy them in big sizes. Really big.

Housing

Many people insist on two incomes so they can afford the home of their dreams. This is a scam set up by builders and estate agents. Houses exist in the real world, therefore they are inherently flawed. Either it is nice and big but next to the motorway, or it has got lots of character, which means it will probably be condemned because of asbestos if you ever try to refurbish it. Useful advice, if you want to live on one salary, came from Francis Bacon who said, 'Houses are built for living, not for looking on.'

If you worry that your husband's income will not support the mortgage payment, you might think about downsizing. I know a family who had to move to a smaller house when they fell into financial difficulties. The children no longer had their own rooms and the husband's office moved into a corner of the lounge. Within months, this family realised it was the best move they could have made. Children were not disappearing to their rooms and parents separating themselves into offices and workrooms. This change in environment actually helped improve relationships between family members, and may have a lasting positive impact long after the children have grown up, something many parents struggle to achieve and worry about desperately.

While you might think you need the storage capacity of a large house, the reality could be that you just have too much stuff. I know of more than one family who have dedicated at least half of their garage to storing toys which the children have forgotten even exist.

They constantly comment that they wish they had a larger garage, when what they probably need is a large car-boot sale.

What is interesting is that the value of a garage as a percentage of the overall value of your house could equal that of an upgrade to your kitchen. So, looking at what your mortgage has purchased, that garage represents just about the most expensive storage space available anywhere in the UK, especially when you consider you are paying interest for the privilege.

Large houses also require more work in terms of cleaning and maintenance. They often have more complicated gardens, also increasing the workload, even for very keen gardeners. I wouldn't go to extremes with the downsizing idea, however. I know one housewife who has a kitchen so small she has to rest pots of food on the floor because she doesn't have enough worktop space. Needless to say, she doesn't enjoy cooking very much!

Toys

When parents comment on how expensive it is to have kids, they always list toys as one of their financial obligations. Manufacturers have convinced us vulnerable parents that children need lots of interesting toys in order to build up synapse connections in the brain, setting the groundwork for brilliant careers as surgeons. Recently, a study in Germany found that in a number of nurseries that had established 'toy-free' days, the children had fewer social integration problems or incidences of poor behaviour than did the centres offering the normal range of educational toys. By removing playthings, territorial behaviour ('This is mine!') disappeared. Play focused on social interaction rather than possessions.

I am not going to be the one to suggest that your children might squabble less if they had fewer toys. I will let you conduct your own experiments.

My mother has been involved in aid missions in Africa and South America. She not only tells stories about babies wrapped in nothing but scarves, she has also noted that these children usually have nothing more to play with than the sticks, rocks and leaves around them. If they are truly fortunate, they might own a doll made from scraps of cloth. Her observation?

'They do great!' They play well with the other children in the village and they can learn all the normal skills humans need in order to function in society. What most scientists and aid workers agree is that children's development suffers most markedly if their diet is poor and when they are physically restricted in experiencing the world around them. Young children who suffer from violent surroundings, who cannot play outside, whether due to traffic or soldiers or drug dealers, will not be able to develop so well physically, socially or emotionally.

So, save your money on the toys. Lobby to reduce traffic, improve school meals, reduce crime and social unrest, then maybe children everywhere will be able to live up to their potential.

Toys are, of course, still useful teaching tools and they are fun. I'm a big supporter of fun. Very young babies, however, don't need very many toys. I took someone's advice when I was pregnant with my first child and actually did not buy a single baby toy. I made her a mobile, and gave her wooden spoons for her to chew on, and giant whisks for her to feel and wave around. For her first Christmas, I spent some money on toys, particularly puzzles, which were slightly advanced for her age. Her motor skills developed so rapidly that she mastered and outgrew the toys in the space of eight weeks. The lesson for me there was to buy baby toys from the charity shop!

When I was growing up, my mother bought my Barbie doll at a car-boot sale. It was the only Barbie I ever owned and I was never envious of the girls with five or more store-bought Barbies. I sewed clothes for her and my mother knitted her pullovers. My parents were not badly off financially, I just didn't need endless dolls and accessories in order to enjoy pretend play. By the time I was nine years old, Barbie was beheaded and regularly thrown up into the willow tree in our back garden. I am sure her fate would have been the same even if she had come straight from the toy shop and if I had owned ten versions of her. View toys rationally when you purchase them. Forget visions of sugarplums and pink-cheeked cherubs cooing with delight. You will be buying toys for years and they may only be popular (or even stay intact) for a matter of months. If you are trying to live on one salary, toys can be a real waste of money.

Be on the lookout too for other families who are happy to pass outgrown toys on to you. Often the toys that neighbours have casually given to me with an off-hand 'Do you think your daughter would like this?' have been roaring successes. One such item is an activity toy that suctions on to a highchair tray. The toy is perfect for taking to restaurants, for entertaining the baby while I am frantically pulling a meal together, and even seems to mesmerise my husband, which cannot be a bad thing. Best of all, it was free. Don't think of such offers as charity. Think, instead, that it would be rude to say no.

Give careful thought to the toys you buy and you can get very good value for money.

Should I save up before leaving work?

From time to time, advice from a number of very qualified financial advisors has been published to help those who are thinking of staying at home. However, the advice I have seen does not often relate well to reality. Here are a few bad ideas I have heard:

Save every penny you can for five to seven years before stopping work

This is absurd. Babies only take nine months to develop and many women don't even decide to stay at home until they are on maternity leave. After the birth, some need to return to work first to discover that being a housewife has some appeal. Many women today are having their first child at the age of 30, meaning they'd have to know they would like to stay home with their child at the very sensible age of 23 or 25. I don't know about you, but at that age financial planning meant measuring the cost of things in terms of how many pints I could buy for the same price. I know still other women who are starting their families young; pregnant by the age of 22. So, hopefully they knew at 14 that they needed to stop buying clothes and compact discs so they could stay home and be a mother. Have you ever met teenagers so sensible?

The financial model that this advice is based on probably looks brilliant on paper, the numbers nicely growing into a rich nest egg. In fact, this is advice we should all follow, whether we're working or not. But we won't because saving is boring when you have got a pay cheque coming in on a regular basis. If you haven't saved anything until now, don't worry about it. Just ignore this advice.

Practice living on one income while you are both still working

This sounds sensible. However, it makes going to work really difficult. What are you going to do, cut off your childcare? Stop commuting? Not dryclean your suits? Furthermore, until you stay at home you will have no idea how your financial needs will change.

It is possibly more instructive to work out what the second income actually pays for, and most of the time it is merely enabling the woman to go to work, while adding little to the family surplus. If there is extra money from the second income you may discover it just pays for things you do not really need, such as a freezer full of frozen dinners, shelves of books you never read twice, holidays that left you jet-lagged instead of relaxed, and two cars that get driven no further than a couple of miles to the railway station every day. Get rid of the hobby or spending habit which is currently eating up your surplus, and like a miracle, you may find yourself living within your means.

Pay the maximum amount into your pension

The problem I have with this advice is that it assumes you won't go back to work. If you can afford to pay the maximum into your pension scheme at work, then go for it. If you need to pay the daycare centre, put your children first. I have yet to meet a mother at home who plans to stay at home forever, but I know many, many housewives who return to work. Some go back after two years, some after ten. Diligence in looking after your retirement needs throughout your life will prepare you for your golden years. However, if you have three months before your baby comes into the world it isn't necessary to cut back your spending money for the sake of a few months of higher pension contributions.

I am not recommending that you just forget about paying into your pension. However, a more balanced attitude towards money and time needs to be addressed. Both you and your husband do not need to be in the rat race in order to be saving up for retirement. Better management of what money is available for saving or investing will build a larger nest egg than money that is ignored, lost or forgotten by two exhausted earners.

Time, unlike money, cannot be regained once it is lost. There are plenty of stories of fortunes that are built, lost and built again within a lifetime. Money is not ephemeral. Time is. Time, once it is spent, is gone forever. If you don't value what you are doing right now, even if you are getting paid for it, you're wasting your life away.

Once you are at home, watching the family finances, you can give proper attention to your money. I personally believe that women at home make the best financial managers for the family, and savings invested can reap higher returns than money handed over to your pension, which is capped and restricted in all kinds of ways. Some people are so slavish about paying their pension contributions that they have in fact overpaid and are basically giving their money away, never to be seen again. Ask your benefits manager at work to explain to you the company's pension policy until you understand it. Don't worry about sounding stupid. Financial types like to feel clever, and are generally happy to share their vast learning.

I know it's one thing to sit down with your pencil and work out how to save money here and cut corners there, but it's altogether another when that second pay cheque just isn't coming in. Surely seeing the change in your bank statements is psychologically damaging?

If you have developed the right attitude, it is not as awful as you might imagine. One professional couple in London who made the leap found that talking about their needs and worries got them through this transition. 'We're not exactly flowing with milk and honey but we aren't stressed. Communication is the most important thing, and remembering that fair is fair.'

In terms of fairness, one difficult aspect of giving up your income may involve giving up your freedom to buy what you like. Once you become dependent upon your husband's income there is a worry that you will have to ask permission before buying anything for yourself. For some women this is a major concern when thinking about giving up their jobs. One mother who has been at home for five years admits, 'I always felt terrible that I was using his money to buy things that I needed and I couldn't have the freedom of spending like I did when the money was my own'.

Many at-home mothers earn their own pocket money through doing odd jobs like babysitting or gardening, working at home or even working part time. Contributing to your own pocket money can be a real esteem booster and frequently helps get women back into the job market full time once they are ready.

Generally speaking, most financial difficulties can be resolved. Many women find their career does not contribute as much to the family finances as they imagined. Money can be saved not just by living more frugally, but also by shifting attention away from material wants and towards emotional needs. Finally, communication with your spouse about money issues is paramount to examining expenses rationally.

> 'Financially it is more difficult, but I soon got used to having to be careful with money. Our life has changed beyond belief since having a baby. You just do different things to amuse yourself; they don't have to cost money!'
>
> *Sam, housewife for 18 months*

Throwing away your past

> 'I feared losing my career most.'
>
> *Heather, home for five years*

For most women today, giving up a career to stay at home feels like throwing away the future. When we were little, the feminist movement encouraged us to take advantage of every opportunity ever denied to our mothers and grandmothers. 'You can be whatever you want to be,' was whispered into our ears, even as we drew pictures of nurses and ballerinas. Our investment in our education was the path to a shining future. Our effort put into building a career, too, would eventually bring unending joy. At the same time, sex education classes taught us that having a baby meant losing all hope of personal fulfilment. So now we are mothers. Now we don't want to work so much. Does it mean we now have no future?

Obviously, this doesn't add up. Life does not end when you become an at-home parent. You do not cease to be an interesting, attractive, educated and valuable person just because you are a mother. You are still a product of every experience you have had, every book you have read, every hardship you have overcome. The difficulty is in keeping up at home the momentum you built while running down the career track.

One of the myths of education and career is that the path you pick determines where you end up. Directing your life is not like shooting an arrow. In archery, once you aim, that's it. But life has twists and turns, rushes forward and grinds to a halt, seemingly beyond human control. As a woman, your life will change form several times, and it will manifest itself in the role you have within your family as well as in the work you take on to fill your days. I assure you, life at home does not have to mean a life of dead ends.

> 'Work will always be there. My baby will only be small for a very short while.' *Dianna, housewife of four years*

Being a 'Good Mum'

> 'I worried about not being a "good enough" Mum to do it full time. Patience is not always my strongest virtue!'
> *Harriet, housewife of four years*

I have heard just about a thousand times from working mothers that they are better parents for going to work, implying that by being home full time they believe they would be poor parents. What does this mean? Two things. Maybe they do not believe they could handle the stress of looking after boisterous children by themselves and would turn into an 'Angry Mum'. Alternatively, they do not believe they are creative enough to stimulate children all day as well as a trained childcare professional could.

There is no doubt that the Angry Mum is a reality. We have seen the advertisements about child abuse. Mothers who let their stress get out of hand are 'Bad Mums' and everyone else gets to stand around clucking about how awful that woman is. Having experienced twice the stress of dealing with a baby who will not stop crying, I know only too well how overwhelming frustration and anger can be. First of all, you are tired. Really tired. Not only have you not slept since the baby was born, but these days at the hospital they make you sleep with your baby right after the birth, so you are not even allowed one night's rest. The last I heard, sleep deprivation could cause not just depression but insanity and violent behaviour. So is it really sensible to tell a new mother to be rational and calm without also offering her any help?

How I got through those hours when I felt my baby was just altogether too demanding for both our good was to separate us. She went into her cot. I went into another room and did something that was just for me: read a book, washed my hair, took a bath, whatever. If she howled for 20 minutes then so be it. She would have been howling whether I was holding her or not! When I came back, usually she had fallen asleep, but if she was still crying then at least I was rested enough to be sane again. The idea is not to punish my kids by putting them in their rooms, but to separate them from me.

If you have to regain composure quickly, put your child where they will be safe and where they are not screaming in your ear – like in another room, or in the car if you are out shopping – and try one of these two energising breathing techniques. It will take about 30 seconds.

BodyFlex is an exercise and fat-burning system developed by Greer Childers. I use this as the foundation of my daily exercise routine, but the most important part of the system is BodyFlex breathing.

- Stand with your feet slightly apart, knees slightly bent. Bend over, resting your hands on your thighs, just above your knees.
- Now, breathe in through your nose – hard! This should be the noisiest, scariest-sounding inhale you have ever made and should feel as if you have been under water for much too long.
- Then, while holding your breath, pull in your stomach muscles – hard! Your tummy should feel concave. Hold this for as long as you can, which may be just to a count of three or four at first if you've never done any deep breathing exercises before.
- Next, release your tummy muscles and exhale hard through your mouth until your lungs are empty.
- Repeat this at least five times, but aim for ten.

The first time you do this, you may feel faint, but keep at it. Breathing this way does two things: it forces a huge intake of oxygen into your lungs and it stresses your heart, making your blood whoosh the oxygen around your system quickly. You can even do this when you think your nose is stuffed up from a cold. Hard to believe, I know, but true. By the second breath, your nose will be clear and you will not have blown your nose all over your carpet either. Jamming all this oxygen through your system also zooms it up to your brain, stimulating the release of endorphins, a sort of 'feel good' hormone which gets depleted when you are depressed or under stress for prolonged periods.

A second breathing technique I like was developed by Dr Robert Epstein and is called Popeye Puffs. Epstein explains that deep breathing helps during periods of extreme stress because 'When times get tough, our first response is to breathe shallowly, which means that we rebreathe excessively . . . The simplest way to assure the right mix of gases in your blood [is] to make sure that you occasionally exhale fully'. When you breathe shallowly you are not allowing your respiratory system to get rid of the toxins building up as a result of your stress.

- First, breathe in normally through your nose.
- Then exhale using a 'double blow', or puffing out hard twice.
- Repeat this at least ten times.

These are only two super-quick ways to regain your composure if you feel you are going to lose your mind. The library, again, has a whole range of books that outline techniques for reducing extreme stress and cutting short anger.

Another way to short-circuit anger or impatience is to be prepared for misbehaviour. Know in your mind what your rules are, whether it is no throwing toys in the hall or only eating when sitting down in the kitchen, and stick to them. If a toy is thrown, playtime is over. If the child gets up (or down) from the table, the meal is over. If these very simple rules are upsetting for the child, they must be tired, so I send them to bed. Older children can be told to sit on a stair or stand in a corner for a short time. Planning your response to testing or fractious behaviour well in advance can prevent you getting stressed.

Another way to prevent anger is to not set yourself up for a contest of wills against your child when you don't have an easy way out. It amazes me, for example, to see whole families going grocery shopping together. The children will be bored, whinging or hyperactive. Dad is trying to corral one out-of-control kid and Mum is explaining to another for the ninth time why just because a pudding is on offer she is still not going to buy it. There is no easy exit here for parents. Threatening to march straight out of the shop is probably what the child wants anyway, but it would disrupt your goal of getting the shopping done, so parents end up not fulfilling their word. The child wins both ways and the parent has lost. Why torture yourself? If Dad is at home, leave the kids with him and shop on your own. Why have 'together' time if it is just going to be stressful and leave you thinking you have bad kids? Supermarkets stink anyway. Why on earth would children want to spend any time there when they could be helping Dad in the garden or playing football with the boy down the road?

Setting yourself up for unnecessary and avoidable contests with your children leads to being an Angry Mum. Know in advance what the house rules are, and if you have to make up a rule on the spot, then stick to your guns. Know in advance what your response to disobedience will be and follow through. This is not just for the good of the children; it is for your own sanity.

'Boring Mum', the one who does not know what to do with active young minds, is just a myth. There are literally thousands of activity books at the library or available at jumble sales for pennies. Further more, young minds can usually make a game of anything. A doctor once asked me what toys my daughter liked to play with, presumably to understand where she was developmentally. I couldn't think of any toys. We play with blankets and cushions, pots and spoons, the dog and other children, doors and chairs and stairs. The great thing is, most of her favourite games were of her own invention and I just play along.

Boredom, anyway, is a good thing. Being able to entertain yourself is a skill and the sooner children learn to find their own interests, the better. Jamming a schedule full of classes and scouts and social engagements does little for creative development, so making yourself a full-time chauffeur for your child is actually unnecessary. One of the greatest gifts you can give your children is to be a Boring Mum: give them time to be a child and stay out of the way.

> 'Being at home has been a really special time. I feel like I am 'growing' a little man; it is such a privilege.'
>
> *Sarah, housewife of one year*

Social stimulation

'I was frightened that I would feel isolated being at home with the baby all day.' *Lonnie, housewife for three years*

Your brain and social life are good things to worry about, because it means you already know you are a creative, intelligent and interesting person. The challenge is directing these strengths on your own into stimulating projects, outside the well-defined and goal-driven atmosphere of the workplace.

Women whose social lives have revolved around their work and colleagues wonder if they will have any friends after making the move to home. The social hothouse of the work environment is difficult to replace. For many women, building up a new social network is a major project in itself.

Lonnie, who lives in Surrey, had this worry. She says, 'I did not realise how many people my child would help me meet and that I would meet people that today are very good and close friends'.

For many people, work is their social lifeline. Sometimes work becomes a life preserver if the atmosphere at home has gone sour. The social importance of our workday cannot be denied. At-home mothers can easily find themselves cooped up with no one but children to talk to. Even worse, husbands coming home from work may offer little relief, either in a poor mood themselves or just too exhausted for conversation. The potential for loneliness is real, and again, the housewife must have a plan for combating it.

One housewife who left a career she loved to stay at home warns, 'Make sure you have lots of friends in a similar position. People do not just come knocking at the door. You have to go out and make friends'.

How you make friends is an interesting problem. Sam was determined, after leaving work, to build up a network of friends right away. 'I had read in lots of books and magazines that it was essential to have "mummy" friends so I set myself the task of actively trying to find these mystery people. At the ante-natal classes I spotted a couple of other girls who seemed on my wavelength and made no bones about thrusting my telephone number at them as they disappeared into oblivion after the last class. I had even nominated myself as the organiser of the aqua-natal class reunion so that I could craftily acquire even more prospective friends' telephone numbers! This really paid off and I have managed to get a sizeable group of mummy friends.'

It does not take too much initiative to get yourself out to coffee mornings or to sign up for classes. Showing yourself in public, though, is only half the battle to making new friends. Shrouding yourself in a gloomy cloud because you think your life has no purpose will not help your social life. In order to attract people to you, you have to maintain your interests – all the things that feed into making you a unique individual. This is important because you will not have your career as a conversational prop anymore and talking only about children, for some women, becomes boring.

This is not true for all women, of course. Children are indeed fascinating and about a third of the women I surveyed have become very involved with their local National Childbirth Trust group. Others have begun seriously studying areas such as paediatric nutrition, midwifery, early development or alternative education such as the Montessori method.

You, however, may not find any of these interesting at all, and instead might like space and time away from anything to do with children. Discussions at coffee mornings or with neighbouring mothers do tend to circle around domestic topics, and steer clear of political debate, for instance. If you look to your social life to be intellectually challenging, focusing your time solely on mother and toddler groups may leave you feeling frustrated. Once you feel bored with your social circumstances, there is a risk that your whole experience of being at home will seem dull. Once you decide that home is uneventful and lonely, you have begun to dig a hole that can get very deep indeed.

Depression, not in its clinical form but in the way that most of us describe those dreadful 'blue' periods, is often tied to losing our way in life. Either we are faced with unbearably frustrating obstacles, long periods of grief, or we have somehow lost our sense of purpose. The antidote to these negative feelings is when we can make progress in our search for fulfilment. Work, however, is not the only vehicle for personal happiness.

In the next several chapters you will begin designing a

challenging, exciting life for yourself built on your own talents and interests. Keeping your mind active will, in turn, keep your social connections healthy. Loneliness and boredom do not have to be a part of your experience at home.

> 'I am but a shadow of my former self. Having a child completely changed me. I'm more outgoing, strike up conversations with complete strangers and have a social circle, albeit revolving around toddler activities!'
>
> *Dianna*

If it doesn't work out, you can always go back to work

There is no shame in telling a prospective employer that you took time out to look after your kids, or even to try focusing on some personal projects. If anything, the person interviewing you will probably be intensely jealous!

If you think you will go back to work after a year or more, being a housewife may free up more time for evening classes or home study. You can come out of your time at home even more skilled than before. I know numerous housewives who have learned more about computer programming, for example, once they left work than when they were sitting in front of a monitor for eight hours a day. Some have gained much more insight into business, as they spend rather more time as a consumer and can see why some businesses succeed and others fail.

Learning valuable commercial skills may lead to an improved salary once the housewife goes back to work, meaning that her time was worth more money at home than at work.

Quite a few mothers who have returned to work have found it relatively easy to find a job. Many employers would rather hire someone with maturity and experience, even if the experience is from several years ago, than a new graduate. My husband, who manages a small staff, comments that the ability to integrate into the company's culture is worth much more than training. Young people, full of self-confidence, can be loose cannons. In their eagerness to get ahead quickly, young people fail to understand that their cockiness is a liability. A woman returning to work after caring for her children is generally much mellower, can handle office politics well, and can continue to function during a crisis. This should not be surprising since she has learnt to do it with one or more small tyrants for years.

And. . . what do *you* do?

My dreams and talents have not been shelved in my decision to stay home. I have in fact found the reverse. Better still, I have uncovered a deeper sensitivity to the needs of my community. This building of respect for the people I meet every day has only bolstered the respect I have for myself, even though I no longer have a title defining who I am. You can call yourself what you like, but I find I have never met with disrespect when I simply declare 'I am a housewife'.

As for what it means to be a housewife, let me quickly dispel some stereotypes:

- I do not spend my day shopping.
- I have not the faintest idea what Oprah or Jerry Springer discussed today.
- I have not gained weight. In fact, I have lost a tremendous amount of weight.
- My brain has not turned to mush. It is probably sharper than it was while I was working.
- I do not spend all my time gossiping with other housewives.
- I do not dress like a slob because I have time to look in my wardrobe.
- I am not lonely.

What do I do all day? Well, I had to write a book to list it all!

2
Leaving work

Before I left work I was offered, at one point, the opportunity to try working part time. My job, however, was dependent upon being available all the time to my clients. I did not believe I could be effective at my job working only part time so, when I left, I decided alternative work arrangements other than full time would just frustrate me.

This is not true for all jobs, and indeed if you have doubts about leaving work you should first evaluate all your options.

Evaluate your options

If you want merely to sample life at home without giving up your career entirely there are four basic options:

- job-sharing
- working part time
- telecommuting
- taking a sabbatical

Job-shares

A typical job-share structure allows two people, usually working mothers, to share desks and responsibilities but on alternate days. When it works, the advantages to employers can be huge, as usually the women no longer qualify for full benefits. Also, these employees are conscious that they have less time to do their work and are actually more productive in the time allotted than their colleagues working full time.

Problems often arise, though, when the workload does not transfer smoothly. One half of the share may not be carrying her weight, making you work harder to compensate. Even when the work is fairly distributed, you will still have to compensate for each other from time to time. For example, one job-sharer will usually have to work full time for several weeks a year while her counterpart goes on holiday. Also relationship problems are not just restricted to that between the two sharers. Full-timers may resent the job-sharer if it interferes with their ability to get things done. Even if the share operates fairly smoothly, full-timers, especially those with family, may feel resentful that someone else is receiving apparently preferential treatment.

If you only want to work because of financial concerns, these problems may not bother you. If, however, you are worried about saving your life's investment in your career, office politics can quickly undermine the job-sharer's efforts.

If job-sharing is an option where you work, talk to others who are already doing the scheme. Encourage them to be honest about both the benefits and disadvantages the system has presented and evaluate their experiences carefully. What may work for one company, one department, or even one couple of job-sharers, may not work at all for you in your situation.

Working part time

If you are concerned about staying on top of changes in your industry or keeping your skills sharp, working part time may be the best solution. I know of one mother of four who worked in the medical profession before quitting to stay at home for her family. Now, ten years on, she is ready to return to part-time work, but a few prospective employers have expressed concern that her technical skills have become rusty. In all other respects, though, they thought she was an excellent candidate. If she had been able to work part time, even just periodically most hospitals today would be competing to hire her.

Happily, she has found, without too much difficulty, an employer willing to help her get her skills up to date. Where there is a will, there is a way, remember. So just being out of the labour market, if that is the route you ultimately take, does not mean you will never be hired again, no matter how technical your profession may be.

Be aware that part-time work is usually only a way to mark time in your career. Do not expect to advance much, or at all, if you decide on going part time. But when you do decide to return to work full time, the effort to keep up to date will be appreciated by employers who may not only be quick to hire you but may even accelerate your career prospects.

In the meantime, part-time work can be frustrating. Many part-time working mothers I have met find either their new role is effectively a demotion or discover they are expected to produce 40 hours of work on a part-time schedule. When you are expected to work part time doing the same job you had full time, you may find, as the months pass, that you are still working 30 or more hours a week, but without any of the benefits of working full time.

Changing employers seems to be the best way to control this tendency for schedule creep. Harriet, who left full-time work after her second child was born, works two evenings a week as Duty Librarian at the local university. The role is perfectly structured for part-time work since the hours and duties required are clearly defined. Another mother I know has started working the evening shift at the local pub. Again, knowing exactly when you are to start and finish work is the best way to avoid frustration and misunderstandings.

If you, presumably, want to cut back your hours in order to spend time with your family, you don't want the demands of your part-time work to encroach on your family time. Make sure you can control both the hours you work and the duties that are expected of you.

A final consideration about working part time is that it can also help you experiment with living on less money, but this isn't universally the case. If you need to commute, wear a uniform or suit, pay for professional childcare or buy a meal while you are working, you may find you are still spending most of the money you earn.

If financial worries are your biggest concern, one of the best ways to keep your income while at the same time reducing your expenses may be telecommuting.

Telecommuting

Telecommuting means working from home and using the telephone and internet to stay in touch with the office. Many jobs lend themselves to telecommuting and the financial benefits to employers can be large, since they do not need to pay the overheads associated with providing a desk for another employee. Productivity of telecommuters is often high, as employees are more conscious of how much time they spend procrastinating. Getting up to make a cup of coffee when you are at home can suddenly seem like an abuse of your employer's trust, whereas at the office you would consider it a right! Telecommuters also do not have to get to work physically, so time traditionally spent on a train reading the newspaper can be used actually getting some work done.

Telecommuting is attractive for the employee not only because better use can be made of time, but also because the costs associated with going to work disappear. Making your own lunch when you are at home does not seem as bad as bringing a sandwich into the office, for example. Clothes for work turn into your pyjamas or jeans and trainers, so the expense of dry-cleaning or buying five pairs of tights a week just doesn't exist. Your childcare costs can also be reduced, but not always. You may find you still need some form of child-minding, but the time spent by your children in daycare may be cut by as much as half. At the same time, you are still able to bring in a full-time pay cheque and also fulfil your desire to be more available to your children.

The downside of telecommuting is, again, jealousy from colleagues. Who wouldn't want to be organising important deals or events while relaxing in their fuzzy slippers? For many, working from home might be their only chance ever to get a desk near a sunny window.

Being physically absent from the workplace makes staying on top of office gossip a real challenge. Workplace chat, as most working women well know, is critical for keeping tabs on political undercurrents. It is difficult to know where the business may be heading, or even if your manager may be on her way out, if you are not actually in the messy middle of office politics on a daily basis.

Being absent from the office can also cause your projects to get short shrift, even from people as loyal as your secretary, particularly if she has to support several other people who can actually stand in front of her and demand attention. Many telecommuters I have met have found it necessary to show their faces around the office on a regular basis in order to make sure their position in the hierarchy is not slipping.

If you manage to avoid becoming invisible while all is going smoothly, you may find you stand out unfavourably during business downturns, making you an obvious target during lay-offs. If job security is important to you, consider the possibility of giving up your home office when the industry environment threatens to become unstable. Also, be prepared for your employers to change their minds about your work arrangement at practically any time, no matter how unfair or irrational this decision may seem to you. After all, your colleagues' view from the office of what you are doing may look very different.

For example, telecommuting arrangements sometimes fall apart owing to the vagaries of technology. E-mail can become a lifeline for telecommuters. If there is a problem with your computer, your ability to work from home may be severely affected, and it can be expensive for companies to send technical support staff out to your house if you have problems. Even when you decide the technological limitations are only a minor problem, the people who are still dragging themselves to the office every day may not see your ability to be incommunicado in quite the same light.

Telecommuting can open up new work horizons, of course, as, if you are willing to try severing ties with your current employer, it lends itself well to home businesses and freelance work. Marketing, public relations, consulting, programming, editing, design work and a variety of other services can easily be provided via computer. If you have an expertise that depends on your intellectual capabilities, it may be worth giving some thought to whether you could set up a home business. If this is an avenue that appeals to you, you'll find that an increasing number of books about home businesses are available. However, setting up your own business can demand a lot of time, which brings us back to the problem of creating time for your family.

One of the main problems of telecommuting, from the point of view of your family, is that it can be hard to stop working. Going to and leaving a place of work sets clear boundaries both to your employer and to yourself as to when you are on or off duty. Working from home, however, holds out the possibility of working at any time of the day or night. This flexibility can be terrific if you have an essentially creative career, since inspiration can strike at any moment. It can also be a nightmare if you are prone to giving your work 110 per cent effort. If you are likely to fall into this behaviour, your wish to spend more time with your family may actually be undermined by working from home.

In addition to your family life, don't disregard the effects that working from home can have on your personality and work style. Research shows that telecommuters generally return to the traditional workplace eventually, and this in itself can cause problems. People who have successfully worked from home learn to become very self-reliant about administrative details, such as when they start and stop working, what constitutes a valid interruption and what can be ignored. Once they return to the traditional workplace they find that being told what forms are needed for filing expenses, what hours they are expected to be at work, and when breaks are permitted, feels not only stifling but obnoxiously paternalistic.

On the other hand, working on your own can seem a burdensome responsibility. Your own guilt can make working at home deeply unpleasant and fraught. Some women report that they worry constantly about losing the respect of their colleagues, that if the phone rings and the baby is noisy or the dog barking this infers a lack of professionalism. *Woman's Hour* on BBC Radio Four related a story about a woman who was so worried about this she stashed her crying baby in the airing cupboard if the telephone rang. Obviously, fear of losing respect can be crippling, causing illogical and very damaging behaviour. This woman, by allowing her insecurities to interfere with her responsibilities as a parent, could easily find a welfare officer taking her child away. If this sounds like something that you might do, look very carefully at your attitude towards work and respect before deciding to intertwine your work and home life so intimately.

The best way to check the viability of telecommuting for your situation is to try working from home perhaps one day a week for a period. See how this arrangement affects your colleagues and clients. You can also evaluate how disruptive it would be to your work to have your children with you at home, and what sort of compromises might have to be made in terms of childcare. Your relationship with work will change if you decide to telecommute as, by necessity, the spheres of work and home often become quite tightly knitted together. If your aim is to free up time to spend with your family while still working full time, telecommuting may not be an appropriate solution for you.

Taking a sabbatical

Taking a sabbatical can be the perfect solution for the woman who is loath to make any drastic decisions about an uncertain future. If you have been working for the same employer for a number of years, there may be a sabbatical policy available to you. If not, you may find your employer is willing to let you take six or 12 months' unpaid leave anyway, and still protect your position.

This option now looks as if it may become more common with the recent passage of the EU directive on parental leave. The UK is still the least generous in this provision, allowing parents the right to a maximum of four weeks' unpaid leave per year for three years. Other EU states allow parents to take a full 13 weeks all at once, at varying rates of pay, so there is pressure to make parental leave a paid right in the UK as well.

Taking a sabbatical can be a refreshing option for employees who feel torn between loyalties. You will not be forced into a decision to leave work altogether, which is difficult enough, and you can try being at home in a healthy, rather than fearful, environment.

One housewife I know warns women who are considering staying at home full time not to 'leap into it naively thinking it will be easy'. Taking a sabbatical allows you to hedge your bets in case being at home is no fun for you after all. If your boss is not able to offer you a sabbatical, he may still be able to promise to try to re-employ you should you find that being at home was the wrong choice.

The most obvious downside to a sabbatical, in my mind, is that you are obligated to return to full-time work. After all, you have made a deal with your employer to take you back, whether the break is a short four weeks or a much longer period of months. Deciding not to return after being granted a sabbatical is not very considerate and can prejudice your employer against offering such special dispensation to anyone else. A sabbatical is a privilege, not a right, as indeed are most flexible work schemes. If returning to work actually does not appeal to you, a job-share or part-time arrangement may be more appropriate for you while you experiment with being at home.

Negotiating special work arrangements

While your company may offer many flexible work arrangements, how happy your boss is about these policies may be another story. If you have a manipulative, insensitive or emotional manager you will need a well thought-out strategy for discussing your wishes. Fortunately, this is not as hard as you might think. People are often surprisingly predictable in their reactions. I have found that I can rehearse an entire difficult conversation in my head and forecast pretty accurately what the other person is going to say at every stage.

The best way to approach a planned conversation is to work out what you want to say, and say it using the fewest possible words. This allows you to remember your 'lines' and it seems to improve the predictability of the response. If you have a tendency to run on and talk endlessly, you will throw off your predictions. Your manager may become impatient or frustrated that they can't respond to you. It is better, in a potentially tense conversation, for you to be the one who is focused and prepared.

Make sure, in your imagined conversations, you try and anticipate the problems your manager will see with flexible work. Surveys show that many bosses have a difficult time visualising how flexible arrangements will work, and see instead only the difficulties. Prepare to solve all his worries. Your ability to accommodate both parties should strengthen your position and you will have a better chance at winning your negotiation.

How you carry yourself is important as well. Don't let your body language convey weakness or worry. If you are asking for some kind of special treatment from your manager it is important to approach the conversation with confidence. A pleading attitude, as if you are throwing yourself on his mercy and only your boss can make your life easy, will probably cause you to lose the negotiation. Gavin Kennedy's book, *Everything is Negotiable*, could be helpful if you find negotiation intimidating or difficult.

The most important thing, however, is to remain upbeat and be prepared for any outcome. You may have to resign, so be sure that the prospect of becoming a housewife is a result you feel okay with. Losing your bid for flexible work should not mean that you burst into tears. This will not help you if you want to launch an appeal later.

If your request seems to catch your manager by surprise or he is not moving towards a decision you would like, let him know you want a mutually agreeable solution. Then suggest, as nothing needs to be decided straight away, that you resume the meeting in a few days so that your employer can consider all the possible options. Your boss should appreciate both your consideration and the breathing space. However, by controlling the timing of the discussion, you still hold all the cards. Pressuring people into decisions is never a good option. You may get the result you want, but your boss may feel you've blackmailed him. Gentle persuasion over time, with reminders as to what would make you happy, tends to work better in the long run.

You may, however, have decided that you do want to leave work completely. In which case, telling your boss becomes a whole different ball game.

Leaving work

Keep in mind that resigning from a job to stay at home is not the same as 'giving up'. Many career women, encouraged to face obstacles head-on and barge ahead come what may have probably also had an upbringing that discouraged giving up at the least little difficulty. However, being unhappy with the balance between your work and personal life is not some tiny little difficulty. If it is preventing you from being effective, either at work or as a mother or wife, this is a real problem.

Being a housewife, remember, does not have to be a life decision. It does not even have to be a career. It could just be a break for a year or two. Resigning does not mean you are giving up, you're just taking a short breather. Even people who climb Mount Everest take long acclimatising breaks on their way up. It does not make them quitters or losers.

No one said it would be easy

Most of the at-home mums I have met, who have experienced life both at work and at home, would support you no matter what you decided. I invited several to give their advice to women like you. Here is what they said:

> 'If you think it is the thing to do and you can afford it, then try it. If you love it, great! If not, then do not feel bad. Being a stay-at-home mum is not for everyone.'
>
> *Lonnie, former administrator in accountancy training*

> 'Make sure it is the right thing for *you* to do. When I had one child, going back to work full time was right for me at the time . . . With the second child I felt very differently.' *Harriet, former librarian*

> 'No woman should be fearful of giving up work. The decision is not irrevocable, and if any woman finds it is not for her she can simply change course again. I gave up work with an open mind, half expecting to be bored witless and to want to go back, but it just did not happen.'
>
> *Kerry, former healthcare operations manager*

> 'Try it and see! It is possible to change your mind again and get another job.'
>
> *Sam, former defence industry commercial manager*

> '[If a woman is frightened of leaving work] she could possibly ask her boss if she could work part time for a trial period. If he appreciates the work she already does then he would probably agree. [Otherwise, she could] take extended holiday leave and see how being at home suits her.' *Kelly, former hairdresser*

> 'If the worries are not financial ones, they can be overcome. It is frightening taking on the whole responsibility for bringing up the children, stimulating them, making sure they learn and grow, but it's also exciting. It's a scary job, but a very rewarding one.'
>
> *Christine, formerly in insurance claims*

> 'It's worth giving up your job, even if it's just for a year to be with your child and help them develop into the kind of person you'd like them to be. They grow so fast and it's an opportunity you may regret missing when they're older.' *Emma, former education degree student*

> 'If [being at home] doesn't work for you at least you know you have tried, which has got to be better than looking back and wishing you had been there.'
> *Mary, former nursery nurse*

If you are thinking of staying at home, try it. Sign up for a six-month or one-year contract. Now, let's write that resignation letter!

Handing in your notice

Handing in your notice can feel like chopping off a limb, sometimes to no good purpose. Becoming a housewife is a total change in role, and one that does not get much good press. It is not like the other times you may have resigned. Most people have another job to go to and can feel their future is secure. Leaving work to be at home can feel like an act of insanity. Once you bite the bullet and hand in your notice, don't be surprised if you feel terrible.

When I resigned from my job I cried every day for three months. I was so frightened that I had made a mistake I telephoned my mother for several days both before and after writing my resignation letter. It doesn't sound like a good way to start a new job, but I was grieving. Mourning the passing of a familiar role can take you through the same stages as someone who has suffered the death of a loved one. This is especially true if you closely identified with your career-woman image.

This does not happen to all women who leave their jobs to stay at home. Some are ecstatic, thrilled with the freedom of not having to answer to someone else's beck and call. For them the joy is immediate, and they are quickly confident that they made the right decision.

Some women find they hate being at home, and this is normal, too. Just like finding a job or boss you cannot stand, staying at home is not for everyone. This doesn't mean the working woman is a lousy wife or mother. Nor does it mean that the working woman is smarter, more ambitious or more creative than the woman who chooses to stay at home. Each individual must find for herself the life that suits her personality and family best.

When the time arrives to confront your boss with the news there are some things you should keep in mind. First, women tend to feel they need to pass on bad news in a face-to-face meeting. This, women believe, shows sensitivity to the person they are letting down and gives them a chance to discuss their feelings.

Men, on the other hand, generally speaking, are perfectly content to mail their resignation notice or leave it on the manager's desk. This does two things. It allows the boss first to absorb the news in private, and then to work out how he will deal with the situation. It also reflects men's ability to distance themselves emotionally from their employer.

Often a person resigns because the employer has let the employee down, so there is no reason for the person resigning to feel they are dealing their boss a hard blow. Leaving to be at home with your children, though, seems to some women to smack of weakness, and they may come up with an elaborate resignation ritual to prove either that they are as strong as ever or that they have been driven to this terrible, desperate result. Neither is really necessary.

Just leaving your boss a note may feel as wimpy as having your friend secretly pass love notes in class, or breaking up with your boyfriend from school over the phone. There is not really a need for confrontation, and if you don't want to face your boss offering you more money or a more flexible schedule, then don't discuss your decision. Just say, either in your letter or in person, 'I'm sure you realise that this was a very difficult decision for me,' and leave it at that. Most people will see that you are drawing a line in the sand you would prefer they stay behind.

Women may feel indebted to their employer for giving them a lucky break. In reality, a person is employed because they were the best candidate for the job, not because the interviewer felt sorry for them. You paid them back for the opportunity by turning up for work every day and doing a reasonable job. They expressed their gratitude to you by giving you a pay cheque. This is how the employee/boss relationship works. If you and your boss are good friends, there is no reason why the relationship can't continue once you leave. Furthermore, your boss as a friend should then be more understanding of your need to try staying at home.

Keep this in mind if you think you are going to burst into tears or feel compelled to buy your boss a present. You don't have to justify your decision with anyone outside your family. Your boss will recover. He will not be haunted with questions of why you left, and whether or not he takes it personally is really not your problem. Companies have been known to go on quite successfully for several lifetimes, regardless of employees resigning, dying or retiring. Believe me, you are replaceable at the workplace, no matter how talented you are. You are not replaceable to your family.

If you do think you will return to work in a few years, former employers are a great place to start your job search, so do try to make your departure positive for everyone involved. Tie up loose ends. Don't leave half-finished projects for your successor to discover weeks after you have gone. Maintain contacts so that you can keep abreast of changes in the business and so that you can send out signals as soon as you want to return to work. Even if your old employers do not have a job for you once you are ready to start working again, they will usually know of vacancies at other companies and can recommend you personally.

Another nice touch is to write a thank-you note to your boss and any other senior managers you have admired. Bosses are often put under a lot of pressure to keep costs down and have to refuse requests from their staff all the time. A note saying you were proud to have been part of their team, that they were an inspiration or even just a joy to work with will make their whole year. Since this chapter of your life is coming to a close, why not give it a happy ending?

3
Now what?

Having dealt with your work-related concerns, we now need to consider what is going to happen when you are at home all day. Working women, being intelligent and action-oriented, do not necessarily relish having their day dictated by the demands of children, pets, mealtimes and cleaning. A major dilemma for women is shifting from possessing a clearly defined job description and understanding how they neatly fit into a business organisation, to being in equal parts master and servant to the people they love.

Understanding the social structure of the family

Home is not work. The organisation of the family should not be viewed like other social structures. Defining what a family is has troubled sociologists and government ministers alike. While it is difficult to say what the family is, we all know one when we see it! Families should not, however, be compared to businesses. Businesses have to compete to survive, for example. A family does not, at least not in the modern era. You don't see men heading off to the supermarket with clubs in their hands, beating off members of competing clans in order to grab the last Styrofoam tray of steak.

Businesses also need things like mission statements in order to understand their competitive position within an industry. Employees or divisions that fail to contribute to that mission in an efficient way will be eliminated. Families don't generally do this; at least not healthy ones. We compensate and compromise, in order that even the least able member of our family can thrive.

In looking at caring for our families in any rational way a new social structure must be defined. This is one reason why the transition from work to home is difficult for women. The concept of hierarchy, service, goal-setting, even budgeting just does not fit when transferred from a business setting to the home.

Misunderstanding this is another reason why women fear leaving their jobs. Children become, in a scary way, transformed into surrogate bosses or clients. If you accept this role for children, you can only see yourself in a servile position. What the boss says goes. The client is always right.

Having had a boss to tell us what to do all the time conditions us to rely on our environment for clues as to what our goal for the day will be. Children, naturally demanding attention, seem to fall very conveniently into the dictatorial role once occupied by your boss or customers. Because children often don't seem rational, care of such surrogate customers can seem to be an overwhelming and potentially unpleasant obligation.

Christine commented that before leaving work she really worried most about 'coping with the children every day, stimulating them enough, and also going brain dead with the lack of adult company'. The media do not help us to allay this fear. Parents are charged with the responsibility of 'stimulating' children's intelligence or creativity. The shelves of books and piles of magazines telling parents how vital this is to a child's future do little to diminish our paranoia that we are the sole arbiters of our children's futures.

Every summer holiday, articles abound about how children drive their parents crazy with demands for entertainment. Your family life does not have to be like this. Children are self-determining individuals, just as you are. When we were little, the compulsion to schedule every minute of a child's day did not exist in society. Two generations ago, it was very normal for a mother at home to give no more detailed instruction to her bored child than to go and play outside. Most of these children did not suffer for the absence of an entertainment committee.

By the same token, being available to your children on their terms is very rewarding. Kelly notes that 'I feel the children are much more educated before going to school by being with me'. Your level of involvement in your child's life is entirely up to you. You shouldn't feel that giving up being a wage slave means becoming a servant to the children.

Husbands, too, get classed in business terminology, pigeon-holed as 'equal partners', 'colleagues', or even in the coveted 'boss' or 'client' role. You must throw all these titles away when looking at your family. Your family is neither composed of tyrants nor invalids. Your motivation to care for them and to let them continue to live in your house is founded on love, though enforced with an innate sense of responsibility. They are individuals in their own right, capable of doing, deciding and achieving many things for themselves. Still, you have a job to do, and it is a service role, but how do we understand the housewife as anything other than a doormat, servant or nursemaid?

I've got a secret. Don't tell anyone, not even your closest friend. I will say it very quietly.

Housewives are leaders.

Housewives are leaders

Yes! But not like Napoleon. Not like chief directors, prime ministers, football coaches or headmasters. You are a leader, but in the manner of Jesus, Lao Tzu or Socrates. First, you are a source of wisdom and guidance. Hopefully, your family turn to you when they need help. Second, your actions and efforts are guided by love and familiarity, meaning that managing the family should follow natural and obvious precepts while requiring minimum effort. Third, you master all the information regarding the household. If your husband wants £5,000 for something, he should be consulting you to decide whether the family can afford it. Finally, you hold the power of delegation. You may manage all the household duties, but they do not have to be accomplished by you.

You are a source of wisdom and guidance

As a mother, this role should be obvious to you. A leader such as yourself doles out hugs, sympathy and a trip to the bakery quite willingly when requested. You very probably already have an open invitation to your family for any help or advice they may need. Vulnerable and honest behaviour is acceptable in children and husbands when it comes to seeking your help. Pathetic, however, would be pushing your role as a leader too far, and disrespectful behaviour should be corrected.

Jesus did not believe, for example, that he had to save humanity. Humanity had to save itself. He offered to show the way. He willingly helped the people who sought him out, but he did not scorn those who rejected him. He, too, offered an open invitation. In this way, you can direct your family not at your understanding of need, but at theirs.

Natural precepts of love and nature guide you

Guided by wisdom, you offer help that is reasonable. If your five-year-old wants to be spoon-fed, his demand for help is unreasonable. As a capable individual, your son would not benefit from having a slave-mother. Lao Tzu, who wrote the *Tao Te Ching*, explains that life is not a struggle, but rather more like steering a boat down river, seeking a natural and co-operative path. Your talents, knowledge and love should naturally adapt to the best interests of the person asking for help.

When your efforts are moved by your talents and knowledge, respect for your role by your family should grow. However, trying to battle against what *is* normal or reasonable, will lessen your strength as a leader. For example, your 12-year-old daughter wants pierced ears and you think that she is too young. If she rails and rages about how awful and unfair you are, she is like turbulence in a river. Giving in and failing to be alert while riding these rapids means you get pulled under, and you lose control. If however, your daughter saves up her pocket money for a year and has been doing research on how to look after her pierced ears, then just as you would follow a clear and straight current, perhaps this demonstration of maturity should be rewarded?

You are the gatekeeper of information

In terms of mastering all the information about the house, don't limit yourself to just knowing the activity schedule and telephone numbers of your children's friends. I highly recommend you get involved in everything, from paying the bills and setting a budget to deciding on investments, insurance and mortgage. The more familiar you are with the finances in addition to schedules, friends and health needs, the more valuable you will be to your family.

By choosing not to know details about your home and family you implicitly give up your leadership. People often wonder where parents' attentions are when their children are found with knives, drugs or stolen property. You don't have to be with children all day long to know what they are up to or how they are doing. As an at-home mother, this responsibility should be easier for you than for a working mother. If you know and demand, as the leader, that you have a right to all logistical information about the house, you should be able to negotiate dilemmas such as the right to privacy, for instance. Are your teenagers smoking in secret? You have a right to know at the very least because it is a fire hazard and because you are obligated as a parent to be concerned for your child's health. If you let your authority as potential knower of all things slip, your leadership role will go with it.

Use the power of delegation

Finally, adapt your responsibilities according to your abilities, and let the talents of others fill in the gaps. I am fine at balancing the bank statements, for instance, but my husband says my overall administrative skills are not great. So we share filing and organisation duties. In this way, I still know everything about our money and where it is and am not ignorant whenever a financial discussion arises. As the reader of statements, I am also the first to know about changes in our mortgage payments, for example, or interest income on savings, meaning I can instigate important financial decisions about changing lenders or banks.

The Socratic method can be useful in this concept. Socrates was known for feigning stupidity with his pupils. He would ask endless, apparently obvious, questions. In the arena of logic, the purpose was to tease out inconsistencies in his opponent's argument. For the purposes of delegation, however, putting yourself apparently second to the abilities of your family members teases out their talents and intelligence.

Either through questioning, silence, observation or listening you can become aware of your child's capabilities. When my daughter became interested in putting small toys into pots and boxes, I began to delegate the process of tidying. When she seemed to get bored at mealtimes and regress in feeding herself with a spoon, I discovered she wanted to progress to using the apparently more grown-up fork.

In involving a child in a lesson, feigning ignorance can be a helpful motivator. When they claim not to remember anything of a history lesson, for example, you could ask 'So, purple bears escaped from the Arctic and ate all the Nazis, did they?' They will then be keen to prove that at least they know purple bears had nothing to do with the Second World War.

The same technique may be useful in gently lecturing older children about sex, drugs or smoking. If they think they know it all, then let them tell you about these topics. They may be receptive to a discussion on why they think these activities are not dangerous, and their comments could give you the opening you need to educate and inform, sharing your love and wisdom while demonstrating profound respect for their intelligence and maturity.

Recognising the leader in yourself

Leaders of course, benefit by having an aim. I believe my job is to create a secure and loving home for my family. I am not a maid. I am not the entertainment committee. I am not a secretary. I manage the household but I am not a slave to it. Easy to say, but hard to do, however. In order to maintain the upper hand in the battle for domestic supremacy, you need to have an action plan.

The first step requires you to take full responsibility for your actions and decisions. This means that when you decide to go on the Wimbledon wheat grass diet, you cannot blame business lunches for derailing your efforts. If you are late picking the children up from school, it is not your mean old boss or a very important client who kept you against your will. When you find out your neighbour could have saved you being conned by a cowboy plumber by recommending their honest, polite plumber instead, the fault is not that you have not seen your neighbour in five years because you are always at work. If driving your children from one appointment to the next means you have no personal time, it is not their fault that you have sacrificed every second of the day to them. Being at home is your show. You are your own boss, so run your house the way you want to.

After accepting full responsibility for how you participate in your family's life, you must determine your priorities to ensure that they do not take advantage of you. Being your own boss, after all, can be fun. While the traditional household tasks of cleaning and so forth need to be done, there is considerable scope for personal development, pleasurable pastimes, and family activities. Because you are the boss, you need to familiarise yourself with how to manage your time effectively, and prioritise both projects and obligations so that you have a balance between work and fun. The housewife needs to be armed with some tricks of the trade to get through the hard jobs, as well as to be aware of how to stimulate her creative and intellectual side when opportunities arise for free thinking.

This is not all about getting organised, or determining the perfect way to clean your house or discipline children. It is about maintaining control. Remember you are a leader, not an administrator! One veteran housewife wanted me to tell you that there is a danger in being over-organised. This is a woman with three children *and* a clean house. Kids, pets, in fact the whole universe outside work, are unpredictable and a lot of fun. Too much organisation puts spontaneity at risk. Aim instead to get a handle on the stuff that is no fun, but do not be obsessive about it. That way you remain in control of the nasties like cleaning and finances, but can hand the reins over to your kids or creative self when an opportunity arises to be a little inspired, silly or reflective. Then the sparkling, interesting, intelligent person that you are can flourish during your time at home.

You can also, in a low pressure way, build up your confidence for the time when you are ready to return to work with joy in your heart. Turning off the career path to head home is less about cleaning than it is about emotional and even spiritual clarity. Leaving work usually involves moving through a state of confusion and certainly discomfort. Dwelling too much on the past is not going to help you move forward, out of the storm. Your aim should be to focus on you and your family as you all are today, here, right now. Only by knowing where you are today can you even begin to start thinking about the future in a rational way.

Of course, being the leader does not mean the world conforms to your will. You must be realistic about your life at home. As with other jobs, some of being a housewife is not fun. A lot of the day may be totally out of control. But knowing your priorities should help you get the unpleasant work out of the way or put out the day's fire quickly. Then, proactive, creative, even personal projects can be pursued. After all, you are still a person, even as a wife, mother and homemaker. You mustn't lose sight of yourself within the family unit.

Your personal development is still key to the happiness of your family. Only by fostering her personal talents can the housewife come into her own. The richness of her personality does not reveal itself in how clean her house is, but in how welcoming it feels, how happy her children are, and in how she uses her free time to stretch her own talents.

I recently asked my husband what made him most proud of me as his wife. He was firstly proud of me in my role as mother. Being a father to happy, growing, healthy children is the light of his life and as far as he is concerned that is all down to me. As a husband, he was also extremely proud of how I used my free time to write, develop computer programmes and teach classes. He knows I do not have much free time, but he loves to tell his colleagues at work about my latest projects.

I did not get into writing, programming or teaching because I wanted anyone to be proud of me. I do it because I enjoy it. While I am not on the career track any more, I feel my use of free time is still good role-modelling for my children. What better way to show the endless possibilities life can offer us than by seizing the opportunities suggested by ordinary curiosity?

If you don't want to attend coffee mornings, you don't have to attend every single one. You don't have to just watch television while doing the ironing. You could be composing a new song or plotting a political campaign. Maybe, while your husband's work shirts are steaming, you are designing new eating implements for toddlers, or deciding which supermarket would be a better financial investment. This is not work. It's fun! By the same token, building a social network will be key to maintaining your sanity. If you have kept up your interests, or are working on fostering new ones, this becomes much easier.

While working on your personal development is exciting, you have to first do some work before you can play. The next chapter deals with the obligations of housekeeping that every housewife must face. Learning effective home management is the foundation, not merely for making your home pleasant, but for making your time spent there worthwhile. A failure to build these basic skills properly will actually inhibit your more wonderful talents. Even if you are fortunate enough to be able to hire a nanny, cook, cleaner or gardener, you may want to read this section. Keeping house can in fact add value to the experience of being a housewife.

4
Getting the worst out of the way

Now you are home. There is no boss to answer to; no clients. You can wear what you like – even your pyjamas if you feel like it. Housewives, however, do not just get to skive off all day. They only get to skive off for part of the day, or maybe most of the day if they are really clever. First, however, they must roll up their sleeves, put on the yellow rubber gloves and do some work.

Being at home, as you are probably aware, is a job, like other jobs. What your priorities are in shaping your role at home I leave up to you. However, I have found distinct peace of mind in having a simple mission: to create a good working environment for myself, and ultimately for the whole family.

The home is still a place where work is done. When people return home from work or school, it is not an instant holiday. Children have chores and homework, while babies have the job of stimulating their brains and bodies every minute they are awake. Husbands may have brought work home, or they may help with the gardening, decorating or cooking. You, too, may be studying or even trying to build a business. The difference is that the home allows one to work in a safe environment, away from the harsh judgements of the outside world.

Most people take their model of the perfect housewife from the television shows of the 1960s. The house was clean, the dishes were washed, the dinner table was always properly set, and the housewife looked fabulous in a dress and pearls. However, I never saw her balancing the cheque book or calling her stockbroker. She was never doing a school run, scheduling playdates for the kids, painting the lounge, checking over homework, or telling an electrician in no uncertain terms that his work was unacceptable. While the job description of a housewife may include many elements, the traditional duties of cooking and cleaning are still critical, if not necessarily major, parts of the role. I would add that keeping the family finances is a third vital duty the housewife should take on.

Before we delve too deeply into the topic of labour, let me assure you that I am an advocate of having as much fun as possible. I approach all my obligations with the mindset that I want to spend as little time as possible on unpleasant activities since they do not add fun to my life. However, doing them reasonably well does help keep stress and guilt at bay, so it is worth investing some effort in getting the household under control.

To put the unpleasant aspect of being a housewife into perspective, a friend of mine from Oklahoma offers this gem of country wisdom: If you have to swallow a bullfrog, then you best do it quick. If you have to swallow a lot of bullfrogs, then you best swallow the biggest one first.

The goal of housekeeping is not to be perfectly organised but to avoid losing total control. As long as you feel in control, you can happily enjoy your free time. Therefore, all the ideas and systems suggested here are just that, suggestions. If your standards of housekeeping are below what your mother-in-law might like, as long as you are not nagging yourself to dust the picture frames or cook fewer frozen dinners, then your standards are just fine.

I would like to note that some women love to cook. If you do, then cooking is a creative outlet for you, something we will examine in the second half of the book. If you do not like to cook, like me, I have some tips on how to spend less time cooking and more time doing what you like instead.

Cleaning

The biggest bullfrog I know is called Cleaning. If you can employ a cleaner, terrific! If you can't, don't worry. There is a system that will both clean your house and create more free time. And if you are not happy with your cleaner, you can fire her and follow this plan to do it all yourself with a minimum of stress.

This system really works. I have a friend, a former banking colleague, who once called me to say her husband wanted to send her back to work because she was useless as a housekeeper. She had a small baby and had no desire to return to work just yet. I told her my system, but she said it would never work for her. It was too simple, and she felt compelled to spend whole days cleaning the house. Otherwise, it just wasn't clean. This is a sign of mental illness in my opinion, but I kept quiet. With great misgivings she agreed to try it for a week. One month later, she announced my system had saved her life, and possibly her marriage. Her husband came home one night and announced the house had never looked so clean.

I'm not one of those people who thinks cleaning can be a spiritual experience. However, I do believe that my family can appreciate living in a home that is loved. Cleaning is a demonstration of that love, and a little love is better than no love at all! Try incorporating cleaning into a mission of creating a place that is pleasant to come home to. You may then find it is possible to derive some satisfaction from cleaning your house. If you find spirituality in that, then great! You have done better than I have!

I have read that some people are inspired by the Quaker belief that God lives through our work, so by not cleaning properly you are not treating God's work with respect. Having studied things 'Quakerly', I have to disagree with this advice on the importance of cleaning. Quakers value simplicity because an obsession with material things distracts the mind from the true task of fostering love in the world. Robert Lawrence Smith writes, in *A Quaker Book of Wisdom*, of his Grandfather Stokes who, as a successful physician and devout Quaker, employed a full staff of domestic servants in the early 1900s. Mrs Stokes, presumably, was not on her knees scrubbing the floor. She was probably involved in the revolutionary founding of schools for blacks or immigrants, or other such productive and life-giving work.

Women have been educated alongside men in Quaker schools since the 1600s, so there has long been an acceptance among Quakers of women's ability to use their talents in making the world a better place. While there is a belief in the need to perform tasks earnestly and well, many Quakers would feel that too much effort put into cleaning at the expense of good works in the community is time, talent and energy wasted. I agree. So the first step to living your life at home well is to stop cleaning so much!

The chances are that you and your children spend the most time looking at the state of your house, while your husband gets to admire it at night and on the weekends, if he admires it at all. I hope, too, that if you and your children are busy doing handstands in the back garden, the hard-water stains on your kitchen tap are not your top priority. Remember, 90 per cent of your cleaning time should be spent on cleaning that revolves around hygiene and only 10 per cent on making the house look good. The more children you have, the more this will become true. However, as your children get older, the more they can help with the aesthetic side of cleaning such as tidying and polishing. Children from the age of 18 months can not only begin to learn these tasks, but also enjoy helping their parents around the house. Don't treat a toddler as a little slave, though. Make tidying seem fun and always reward the effort with profuse thanks and kisses.

Hygiene tasks which will probably remain in your domain for years, however, include laundry, mopping up, hoovering, cleaning the dishes, emptying the kitchen bin, changing the sheets, and scrubbing bathrooms and kitchens. If there is someone with allergies, dusting, and scrubbing mildew and mould, will probably be included in this list. Aesthetic tasks for most people include dusting, window cleaning, sweeping the front path, general tidying, and scrubbing mildew and hard-water stains.

To get a handle on the housework you want to accomplish throughout the year, write down the cleaning jobs you feel compelled to do. Bundle these tasks into four-and-a-half manageable to-do lists, one for each day of the week. The half list is your light day, but it won't be all the time. This slack day allows for any catching up on unfinished tasks from the week, or for doing a monthly or seasonal cleaning duty, like taking the curtains to the dry cleaners or washing windows.

This system allows you to put away your hoover on Monday without getting obsessed about when you will get around to scrubbing the toilets. This is because toilets are scheduled for Wednesdays. If I have to miss a day for some reason, I reshuffle the tasks across just four days or double-up duties on one day of the week. Or, I just skip the task that week, knowing that floors or ironing will come up on my list again in just seven days' time.

Make cleaning the house the first activity of the day. Hoovering and mopping are easier when toys haven't been scattered around. Don't worry about perfection except for the hygiene issues that drive you crazy. My particular bugbear is clean dishes. If anyone attempts to help me by washing the dishes it is almost guaranteed I'll end up washing them again myself. I don't even wait for the kind volunteer who washed them in the first place to leave the kitchen. If I spot a dirty glass my brain goes into overdrive and they are elbowed away from the sink. I hate dirty dishes. All other measures of perfection, like hoovering under the sofa, may happen on my slack day or not at all.

Some people feel nap time, if you have young children, is the best time to clean, but nap time is usually my free time. I would hate to give that up just to get a sparkly kitchen floor.

The aesthetic duties, tidying in particular, should happen straight after the toddlers go to bed, or before your husband comes home if your children are older. Do not attempt to tidy up after toddlers while they are awake. It is a pointless waste of time, which will make both you and your children unhappy.

If you feel that you spend your entire life tidying, it's probably because you do not have something more enjoyable to do, but it may also stem from your family not using the house to its full potential. Tidying will be easy once you have reordered your home so that you are using it properly. This is a fun project, and we will discuss using your home in the next chapter.

This is my weekly cleaning schedule:

Monday:	Sweep, mop up, hoover and dust ground floor. Children's washing.
Tuesday:	Hoover and dust upstairs. Adult laundry, except work shirts.
Wednesday:	Clean bathrooms. Wash work shirts overnight.
Thursday:	Ironing. Empty rubbish bins. Take rubbish out for Friday collection.
Friday:	Change and wash sheets. Clean kitchen floor, appliances and wash tea-towels.

Friday is my slack day, though sometimes I find Thursday is quite light as well. Tasks that happen every day, even at weekends, are the washing-up and tidying. I find I can usually complete my work in 30-45 minutes. Notice that I leave my weekends free of cleaning jobs. Sometimes there is unavoidable cleaning that has to happen, either because visitors are coming or a child has made a big mess. This is just enough cleaning for a weekend, which is time I want to be spending with my family.

To motivate myself for the nastiest of tasks, which is cleaning the bathrooms on Wednesdays, I arrange to go to my neighbour's house for coffee as soon as I hang up my gloves. I could cheat, but having the toilets clean while someone is brewing me a cup of coffee in the same morning is quite a treat compared with just coffee all by itself. As a result, instead of dreading Wednesdays, I look forward to them, toilets notwithstanding. My husband has been trained to exclaim 'What lovely clean sinks!' when he comes home on Wednesdays, which is another silly incentive to clean the bathroom.

One housewife I know finds she can spend an hour cleaning one bathroom. If you are like this, and find it satisfying to get the bathroom absolutely pristine, perhaps dedicating one day per week to the bathroom will help make cleaning more manageable.

The point is not to do all your cleaning in half an hour and then fret that it isn't clean enough. Clean to satisfy your own standards. On some days it will take longer, while on others (usually sunny ones) you will be satisfied with running a hot wet rag over all the worktops so that you can rush out and enjoy the weather.

What is important to remember is that housekeeping does not have to take a lot of time however you divide up the tasks. A housewife I know says, 'After having my second child we paid for a cleaner for three hours a week. Having seen what she did in three hours made me realise housework doesn't have to take forever. I try to do most of the cleaning on a Monday, then it's done for the week. I run the hoover round most days, but do a proper job once or twice a week. I am blessed with a dishwasher which I would thoroughly recommend!'

Kerry, a veteran housewife in Surrey, was kind enough to pass on her system. 'I drew up a cleaning roster of daily tasks and a washing rota. I work through them as quickly as possible each day (usually between 10 and 11 o'clock when *Teletubbies* and *Tweenies* are on TV). I prioritise them so that dishwashing, emptying the rubbish and wiping down the kitchen surfaces come at the top of the list, and watering the plants comes near the bottom. I do what I can in that hour and then forget about it. The most important jobs get done, and all my houseplants are dead!'

It is also worth remembering that cleanliness is not the most important part of being a mother. Lonnie says about her cleaning, 'I do the cleaning when I feel that I have the time to do it. I don't worry about there being crumbs on the floor or dirty plates in the sink. I don't think that is important. My mother-in-law taught me the following, and I often think about it:

> If the Lord on Judgement Day
> Asks me 'DID you clean your house today?'
> I shall answer 'I did NOT . . .
> I played with my child and I forgot.'

You may have to experiment with a number of schedules before finding one that works for you. I have found this system to be a godsend. I hope it performs wonders for you too.

Another way to minimise time spent cleaning is to put a little thought into preventing mess in the first place. In my research into cleaning, I found the best tips concerned prevention.

- To save on cleaning the cooker top or worktop, use pots large enough that the contents won't boil over, and use big mixing bowls with deep sides so the mixture doesn't whizz across the kitchen with enthusiastic stirring. If you have a dishwasher, place spoons and other utensils on a cutting board or small plate while cooking, not directly on the worktop. If you have to wash dishes by hand, use a piece of folded kitchen roll instead of a dishcloth. When you have finished, you can use it to wipe up any spills before throwing it in the bin. One second spent preventing mess can save ten minutes cleaning it later.
- To save on washing up, try to make suppers that only dirty one pot or casserole dish. If you are making stew, for example, use a nice large stewpot, and brown the meat and onions in the

pot before adding other ingredients. This saves dirtying a frying pan. Many people love their steamers, but I find the pain of cleaning steamers outweighs the time saved cooking. Try, instead, baking food wrapped in foil so that it cooks in its own steam. The foil goes in the bin after cooking and there is no washing up.

- To save on hoovering, place doormats both inside and outside the door. Research, if you can believe it, has shown that dirt and moisture will finally be removed from shoes after four paces on a carpet. I can't speak for you, but I don't want a doormat extending six to eight feet into my hallway. Just make your family wipe their feet on both mats, and you'll be most of the way there. Someone also pointed out to me the distressing fact that husbands and schoolchildren have to use public lavatories during the day and they are going to trail that stuff home on their shoes. So, perhaps these members of the family in particular should be asked to leave their shoes at the door when they get home, saving you from both dirt and germs.
- One housewife I know uses car wax in her bath and shower to prevent hard-water stains and mildew. Be very careful, however, not to get the wax all over the bottom of the bath, as it can make the surface very slippery. Reapplication of the wax occurs maybe once a year, if she remembers.
- Let cleaning agents and tools do the work for you. If you spray bathroom or kitchen cleaner on a spill let it sit for a few minutes before wiping it off with a cloth. These cleaning agents, combined with water, dissolve dirt and grease into particles and float them off the work surface, ultimately allowing you to wipe it clean straight away. However, they need time to work. So spray, make a cuppa, and then come back to wipe up.
- If you use a scrubbing brush with plastic bristles on your dishes, do not press hard. Press gently. The abrasive work you want from a brush comes from the tips of the bristles, not elbow grease. You can feel the difference by pressing a scrubbing brush against your hand. Scrub hard, and the bristles, pushed flat, are completely smooth. Pressed only lightly, you can feel the brush scraping at your skin.

I hope these tips recall the idea of Lao Tzu: to achieve maximum progress with the least amount of effort. Cleaning is not a life, so why waste time doing what you do not have to?

Finances

You, as the leader of your family, should be intimately familiar with the household finances because as knower of all things you need this information to make intelligent decisions, whether it concerns buying Christmas presents or being able to cope should something happen to your husband. It doesn't take a lot of time and you can help to manage or even increase your family's wealth. Now that is power!

If you are a housewife who manages the household finances, you need an office. It can be a box or a whole room, but it needs to hold your cheque book, a book of stamps, a calendar and a pen. When the mail comes in, open it, throw out every irrelevant scrap of paper (no, not the bills!), sort it into statements and bills and then stick it all in your office. Pick one day of the week when you will balance your books. I pick Monday. It usually takes me 15 minutes to do my financial work for the week.

Some housewives only deal with the family finances once a month as the bank statements arrive. If you are in good control of your money, you may only need to look at your finances this infrequently. I have to tell you, however, that rich people do not ignore their money for so long. Some look at it daily, or every other day. If you do not have a grip on your finances or are deeply in debt, I highly recommend you devote a few minutes each week to working out where that money is going. Just as improving your diet requires taking stock of what you are eating today, setting up a realistic budget requires you to know what you are doing with your money right now.

Every week I make a list of my credit card charges, which means I carry the receipts around in a little pocket in my handbag until Monday morning when they are taken out and brought to the office for accounting. This may seem a pointless exercise, but it reminds me on a weekly basis how much money I am spending and on what. Many people recommend paying for things only with cash to avoid the credit card trap. The great thing about credit cards, though, is that they provide an organised record each month of where your money has gone. This is very useful when developing a budget. In our house we use very little cash. Personally I only use cash to pay for parking. Everything else goes on the credit card, which gets paid off in full each month.

After noting my charges for the week, I balance my cheque book against my bank statements, or my charge list against my credit card statement, if I have received it. Finally, I write cheques for the bills that have arrived in the past week. When they are prepared, I write on the envelope the day they are to be posted in order for them to be paid on time. The bills are then paper-clipped to my calendar for the week they are to be posted. This is also a good time to review your budget and determine how much money you can spend that week. Looking at my finances each week helps keep me aware of how we are doing financially, and in fact relieves a lot of stress.

If the mere fact of stress relief will not encourage you to get a grip on your finances, maybe concern for your health will. That's right. Living within your means can help you live longer and in better health. Research conducted by the University of Ohio linked high levels of credit card debt to health problems. They believe that financial stress can affect your health and possibly shorten your life. If you want to grow old and see your great-grandchildren, how about taking a little look at how you stand financially and make an effort to start living within your means?

Looking at your bank balance frequently also allows you to make intelligent purchasing decisions on the hop. We had been needing a full-length mirror in our house for some time. The situation was grave. I had been forced to rely on my husband's questionable judgement of whether the top and bottom bits of my outfits worked together for nearly a year. One afternoon, zooming through a village in our car, I spotted my free-standing mirror tucked away in the back corner of one of a series of antique shops.

'Mirror!' I shouted.

'How do you see this stuff?' Men. They just don't know how to shop, do they?

'What is this village?' I carried on, ignoring him. 'I'll come back tomorrow.'

That's the thing with antiques, isn't it? You have got to buy the item you want as soon as you see it. It's not like shopping at Argos.

The next day I went to the shop. In buying antiques I usually try to work out how much I would spend on a piece before I even inspect it, setting my budget in advance. After examining the item more closely, I try to guess how much the dealer paid at auction, how much they might have had to refurbish it, give them a little profit margin and then finally make them my offer.

It would have been vastly cheaper, of course, to walk away and buy a modern free-standing mirror for one-tenth of the price, or a wall-mounted mirror for even less. However, working through my love test, even though I did not love the asking price one bit, I decided I could love the price over a useful life of 20 years. The mirror was beautiful and very large. The detail was exquisite, and the craftsmanship was solid. This was not a mirror I would get rid of because it was ugly. It was a showpiece.

Because I knew how much I had charged that month on my credit card, how much we had in reserve in other accounts, and what expenses for the house could be delayed for a month or more, I agreed to purchase my mirror.

As soon as I came home, however, I checked my figures again, just to be safe. I had left the dealer a deposit, so I could always back out of the transaction, giving myself a week's cooling-off period.

Knowing the state of your finances well prepares you for the unexpected, will help you manage your debts, and can put you in a strong negotiating position. Many craftsmen respect a customer who knows her financial limitations. A bolshy 'I'll only pay £50 for this' is less effective than an honest 'I love this, but can only afford £50 today'. This signals that you have no flexibility on price. If they want the sale, they just might be willing to work with your budget.

Managing the household finances is not just about saving money at the grocer's or on the children's clothes. Knowing the state of your finances puts you in good stead for negotiating all the major expenditures your family faces every year as well, ranging from home repairs to Christmas shopping.

As the housewife, you will be spending the bulk of the family money, and not just on food and clothing. You will probably also handle buying furniture and overseeing building work projects.

Simply looking for special offers is not effective if you do not know how much money there is to spend in the first place. You might spot three sales in the high street with three different bargains you think your family needs and purchase all of the items. In reality, you may only be able to afford to take advantage of one of those sales.

My husband and I have an annual review of the major expenses we expect or want to make over the next 12 months. These include decorating, travel and even our Christmas budget. Knowing well in advance what we expect to need enables us to deal with special offers intelligently. When we come across sales, I always ask how long a sale will go on. There is nothing wrong with telling the salesperson that you cannot afford to buy the children new furniture this month, but will have more money next month. They may be willing to give you a discount or to backdate your order form so that you can get the price you want when you want it.

Many sales can be anticipated, and shopping out of season for big purchases can save you a lot of money. The home improvement season, for example, is typically in the spring, so the best time to order a new fitted kitchen will be in December and January. You don't have to have it delivered in the winter, though. When we purchased our last new kitchen, we booked delivery four months in advance, which the salesperson had never seen before. We saved a tremendous amount on our kitchen and had it installed when we needed it and could afford it.

There are also key times of the year when you as a buyer can hold tremendous bargaining power. The best time to buy a new house, for example, is in the winter, usually because the sellers have to move and so are keen to entertain any interested buyers. On the other hand, the best time to buy a new fireplace or heating system is in the summer. We last shopped for a fireplace in July and the salespeople were desperate to do us a deal.

Major building work is also often best scheduled during the winter months, because workmen are generally more available. When we were refurbishing our last house, we had to compete for workmen with the Millennium Dome and the Jubilee Line in London, which were paying outrageous wages. We spent a great deal of time working through the timing of our projects to make sure we got the best price for the work that needed doing.

Shopping in advance like this requires intimate familiarity with your spending habits. You will need to be researching large purchases months in advance of the sale seasons and budgeting your funds appropriately. If you do this, you can actually control your debts since you will avoid racking up expenditures on your credit cards, which take years to pay off.

Timing such major purchases is where all your hard work in planning and budgeting will pay off. Did you know that if you take out a personal loan or charge a major purchase and take five years to pay it off that you will have increased the ultimate purchase price by at least 40 per cent? What good is a 10 or 20 per cent discount if you end up paying over the odds in interest charges?

Home improvements can add value to your house and improve the quality of your life, but you don't have to dent your wealth in the process. Plan these expenses well in advance, look for good deals and pay for things as you can afford them, not just impulsively when you want them.

Some housewives are also involved in the family insurance, refinancing the mortgage, even managing investments. In our house we discuss all of these in detail, but it is down to me actually to act on our decisions.

You mustn't let money frighten you. Confronting your fears and your finances can protect you. While I hate to assume that my marriage (or anyone else's) will end in divorce, I strongly recommend housewives make themselves intimately familiar with the household finances. If a split must occur, you will be on a much better footing if you know what assets there are, and therefore to what you may be entitled. Furthermore, any shady activity always involves money. If a husband is involved in an affair or developing a drug or gambling habit, he will have to fund and organise it somehow, and credit card statements or phone bills can be the first hard evidence that something unpleasant is going on.

Ignorance may be bliss, but information is power. Inform yourself. Read your statements and open the bills. It could protect you.

Cooking

Cooking poses a big problem for many families with small children and hard-working husbands. If your husband, like mine, works long hours, there is no way the children are even going to be awake by the time he gets home. This splits suppertime at least into two cooking sessions. For mothers trying to lose their pregnancy fat, cooking supper twice a day can be an irritating temptation.

I have asked every mother I know how she deals with this problem and have yet to hear one person announce a solution with which everyone is happy. In the interests of diet, many mothers eat with their children. But letting your hard-working husband eat by himself every night seems a little bit unfair. Some housewives even let husbands just forage for their own suppers.

I am a 'non-cook'. Some people love cooking for their families. I am not one of them, and neither are any of my friends. So I classify cooking as work which takes up my time. If this doesn't describe you, you are a lucky woman, so just skip over this section.

However, there are a lot of non-cooks out there. Here are just some of the responses I have received from housewives on the topic of cooking:

> 'What's cooking?!!'
>
> 'Cooking is a bit of a nightmare.'
>
> 'I don't particularly enjoy cooking but I do like eating, so it's a necessary task!'
>
> 'I hate cleaning more than words can say, but I hate cooking even more.'

Many women's magazines devote a substantial number of pages to food and recipe ideas. Considering that most people have a core menu of just 10 to 15 meal combinations, I personally believe the media has invested far too much interest in food. I would read a women's magazine with recipes that toddlers will eat, otherwise I'm not interested. I love a nice meal, but I would rather someone else cooked it, and preferably not in my house so I don't have to clean up.

If you enjoy cooking, that is terrific for you and your family. If you do not, then between you and me, there is nothing wrong with sausages for supper. If you are a non-cook like me you have other talents and there is no reason to waste time doing something you hate. Saving time and fending off starvation while sticking to a budget does require you to cook strategically. And what you cook depends on whom you are cooking for.

Cooking for children

At every opportunity, exercise your powers of delegation. Pre-school children, for example, can prepare their own lunch if you let them. If they like egg or tuna mayonnaise, then keep a big bowl of it in the fridge and let them spoon it on to savoury biscuits or bread. Older children, of course, can wash and select fruit, slice cheese for a toasted sandwich and make just about any cold sandwich they may want. Keep plenty of sliced cold meat and cheese ready for them in the fridge on a low shelf and let them sort themselves out during the day. You could even invite them to make your lunch too, telling them all the while that they make the best sandwiches you have ever tasted. They may start to take pride in building ever yummier lunches for you the more you boost their confidence, and that can only create more free time for yourself. Babies, though, are not so self-sufficient; still you can start them on the road to independence at a pretty young age.

For feeding my baby, I have encouraged her desire to feed herself, even if it means she is eating with her hands. This means she can be feeding herself some fruit chunks while I am working on boiling pasta or whatever the main dish is going to be. Babies, aged between nine and 15 months, become interested in copying their parents. Use this to your advantage and keep alert for clues that your child is ready to move from bottle to beaker or from fingers to cutlery. I noticed my baby became more interested in using her training cup when I sipped my own drink during her meals. After all, Mummy and Daddy do not drink out of bottles. If you can eat meals together, you are more likely to see when your baby is receptive to using a spoon or fork on his own. Their attempts are likely to be messy at first, but practice makes perfect. The sooner they can manage feeding themselves, the more freedom this gives you.

Meal planning

Baby food manufacturers are not superior to mums when it comes to providing nutritious meals. If that were the case, the human race would have died out long ago. Jarred dinners have only been available for the past few generations, after all.

Even though I dislike cooking, I dislike tinned baby foods even more. They don't taste at all nice and don't have any texture. We have been conned into thinking that modern science can produce better food for babies than mothers' home cooking. Once babies come off tinned food, they will have to eat your cooking anyway, so they may as well start developing a taste for the things you are willing to prepare for them.

When planning the baby's meal, I simply make sure there is some protein, a starch, a vegetable and a fruit. If there is any iron-rich food in the meal, it is important to have a fruit or vegetable high in vitamin C, key to natural iron absorption. This is much easier than it may sound, even keeping the finger-food concept in mind. Below I have listed some foods high in iron and foods high in vitamin C. You can mix and match the lists to come up with healthy meal combinations. Spinach, which has both iron and vitamin C, should be treated as an iron source and supplemented with another source of vitamin C, such as fresh chopped tomatoes or lemon juice.

Food combining for natural iron absorption

Sources of iron	*Sources of vitamin C*
Red meat	Blackcurrants
Liver	Strawberries
Kidney	Oranges and other citrus fruits
Black pudding	Cranberries
Mussels	Kiwi fruit
Tinned salmon and tuna	Melon
Smoked mackerel	Pineapple
Pilchards	Tomatoes
Turbot	Green peppers
Egg yolk	Spinach
Soya milk	Broccoli
Peas and beans	Cauliflower
Spinach	
Treacle	
Chocolate	

If you are breastfeeding, paying attention to such combinations yourself will help maintain your health and energy. You can take iron tablets instead, but many women find they can upset the stomach or cause constipation. Why not try getting your nutrients the way Nature intended: from our food and not from a pharmaceutical company? In either case, the last thing you need if you are looking after a baby is a case of anaemia setting in, which will make you tired, prone to bruising, inhibit your immune system and even cause fainting. You don't need to be falling over and banging your head while looking after a newborn baby, so do everyone a favour and eat an egg every once in a while.

The great thing about meal planning for babies is that they will happily eat the same thing every day for lunch without complaint. Don't get hung up on variation, particularly if your baby is still on formula or follow-on milk. A good proportion of her vitamins will come from drinking the formula milk. Once they are toddlers, children will probably only want a predictable meal for lunch anyway, so being in the habit of offering a balanced meal, even if it is the same every day, will ensure that your child is still getting all the necessary nutrients. What is great about this fact is that it means it's not necessary to spend a lot of time planning meals for children if you don't want to. In our house, every meal is pretty much a crisis in this regard, so I keep the larder well stocked for emergencies.

A sample emergency lunch (meaning I have had no time to think ahead and the baby is screaming, obviously dying from starvation) consists of banana or melon sliced into sticks, boiled peas, whole-milk yoghurt, and buttered toast or a cereal bar sliced into soldiers. The only thing I help the baby to eat is the yoghurt and I can spend much of her lunch time doing something other than feeding or cooking, like eating my own lunch!

An emergency supper (which is really a daily occurrence, but it surprises me every evening) could be leftovers from our supper, or pasta with any number of the following toppings: cheddar and tuna, beef bolognaise sauce, canned tomatoes with garlic and any other canned veggies in the cupboard, or spinach and cheese puréed. If she is still hungry, there is always fruit and baby yoghurt to fill her up.

The jury remains out on whether grazing or strict mealtimes are better for children, but I find it easier to cook healthy meals than to remember from one snack to the next what a child has eaten that day. As more research is done on food combining and its effects on health, it may show that meals are simply the most efficient way for humans to absorb nutrients from food.

Because of the effect of sugar on a young baby's teeth, and because it is a challenge to brush their teeth, avoid serving puddings except on very special occasions. You could end a meal with a tooth-friendly snack like raw apple or carrot grated or sliced into sticks, depending on how many teeth your baby has. The roughage acts as a natural toothbrush, cleaning away sticky bits of food left in the mouth.

Likewise, instead of offering biscuits as a snack between meals, try dried fruit or bananas. If you have to carry snacks around in your handbag, these two options are just as portable, though dried fruit offers the advantage that it will not go off if you forget and leave it in the car for a week. These snacks are also very filling, more so than fresh fruits like apples, and for picky eaters, do not taste funny at room temperature. Make sure, for under-one-year-olds, that dried fruit is not sweetened with honey. Honey contains a type of bacteria that can be harmful for some small babies.

Keeping mealtimes relaxed

If you can manage to eat meals with your baby, she will not only be motivated to eat more of her meal, she will learn that mealtimes can also be social. One game my baby loves is to feed Mummy. When she picks up a piece of fruit, I will open my mouth and cry like a starving baby. She carefully feeds me the food and squeals with delight when I take it. This game is fun for babies because it puts them in control of the feeding for a change.

One final tip for minimising mealtime frustration is to let children decide when the meal is over. If they are dropping food over the side of the highchair, they are obviously not hungry enough to eat, so just end the meal. Some scientists studying eating problems in older children believe that 'food issues' are developed during infancy from being forced to eat when they were not hungry.

Overall, do whatever it takes to reduce tension for both you and the children. If they don't eat every single meal in a day, then don't cook elaborate dishes for them. Many mothers recycle meals. If lunch is refused, then it is wrapped up and put in the fridge until suppertime, or pulled out for an afternoon snack. It gets nuked in the microwave and is the only option offered. This is not a special kind of torture for kids refusing their food. It is a refusal to waste perfectly good food. If you made yourself a delicious sandwich, but found you could only finish half, you would wrap it up for later or for your husband to eat, right? If a dish is refused two meals running, only then will I throw it away, as constant reheating only speeds up the spoiling process.

A small child has never in recorded history ever starved herself to death out of stubbornness. So as long as your child is growing and your doctor does not seem concerned, it doesn't matter if your child is not eating at every single meal.

If your child is old enough to communicate preferences, it is good practice to offer an option of two items. Ask if she would prefer a tuna or cheese sandwich, for example. Small children are not often capable of coming to a decision when the options are unlimited. You may find if you merely ask the child what she would like for breakfast, she will select something inappropriate, like ice-cream, and your refusal will just frustrate her. Because you do not want to stand around for 10 minutes while your three-year-old decides what she wants, limit the options to two. If there is no option, do not ask the question.

Cooking for husbands

Husbands can be just as difficult as children when it comes to meals, with the added complication of wanting to eat something different every night. I have found that there is less frustration all around when my husband's input into the issue of cooking is kept to a minimum. I only ask my husband what he would like to eat when I am coming up with my shopping list. He cannot announce in the middle of the week that my stir fry is a disappointment and he wants steak. The only time his interference is allowed is if he phones in the afternoon offering to pick up a curry or to cook supper himself. Indeed, this sort of display of initiative is encouraged!

In the interests of maintaining variety, I have discovered several shortcuts.

Fast food

The fastest way to cook meat in many cases is by frying, and any of my 'proper' meat-and-potato-type meals are fried. Frying has received a bad reputation in recent years because of the fat that often gets added in the process. However, if you keep oil in an atomiser or spray bottle normally used for watering plants, you can coat a pan evenly with a nice thin coat of oil. Three squirts will provide less than a teaspoon of oil but allow easy frying of anything, including meat.

The best way to dry fry meat is to leave it alone, not stir it around the pan or constantly flip it while it is cooking. Turning food too often slows cooking and can prevent meat from searing properly, causing juices to run out and drying the meat. So if you are frying a beefburger, spray a bit of oil on to the pan, get it nice and hot, throw in your burgers and don't touch it for five minutes or so until you are ready to cook the other side.

Chicken, with its versatility, is the king of easy cooking. Cut chicken breasts into three long strips before putting them in the freezer. Try to arrange the strips so they do not freeze together in a big clump. These slices can be put, still frozen, in a 200°C/400°F/Gas mark 6 pre-heated oven for just 20 minutes. This is a huge time-saving from defrosting and then cooking full breasts for an hour or more. **Be very sure the oven is pre-heated, however, or this won't work and the chicken will not cook all the way through.** Alternatively, the chicken can be thrown into a saucepan of sauce and simmered for 15–20 minutes: again, no thawing required. However, if you are unhappy cooking with frozen chicken, these strips will thaw quickly if placed in a plastic bag and in a sink of hot water for about 15 minutes – just enough time to fully preheat the oven, actually.

Fish fillets are also incredibly easy. One tasty method is to fry thin fillets in a little butter, five minutes per side. While doing this, I microwave spinach in a lightly covered glass bowl for three minutes on high. Let the spinach sit for one minute to continue steaming before serving. Alternatively, wrap fish fillets and some good steaming vegetables such as courgettes or French beans, with some chopped tomatoes, some butter and whatever herbs you like in foil, sealing all seams. Bake in a pre-heated 220°C/400°F/Gas mark 6 oven for 20–25 minutes, depending on the thickness of the fish. Throw on some rice or heat up some garlic bread while the fish is cooking. This meal is very easy and there are no pans to clean.

For children, poaching fish in milk is also quite fast. From frozen, I place a fillet in a small ovenproof dish, cover half-way with full-fat milk and bake in a pre-heated 200°C/400°F/Gas mark 6 oven for 30–35 minutes. Drain off the milk after baking and use to make a white sauce with a tablespoon of flour, a knob of butter and some herbs or Worcestershire sauce, nutmeg and ground black pepper. If the fish is fresh or thawed, cook it in the milk at 180°C/350°F/ Gas mark 5 for 10–15 minutes.

I highly recommend that you incorporate fish, particularly salmon, into your diet. New research has indicated that fish, which contains omega-3 transfatty acids, is indeed brain food. Adding fish to your diet, even for only one meal a week, could lower your risk of heart disease and depression, while possibly reducing aggressive tendencies. Housewives need all the patience they can muster (and who needs an aggressive husband?) so if fish will do the trick, it's not a hardship.

The fastest way to cook potatoes, in my opinion, is to boil very small new potatoes. The smallest, which are slightly bigger than a £2 coin, can be cooked in 15 minutes at a rolling boil. Larger potatoes, though, are cheaper, but if left whole take about 30 minutes to boil. To cut time and save money, leave the skins on and chop into quarters or thirds. This way the cooking time can be cut again to 15 minutes.

Steaming is widely touted as the healthiest way to cook vegetables, and I'm a great fan of this method. What I don't like about steaming is that it usually dirties two pots and can take up valuable time, especially if you have a screaming child (or husband) to feed. Recipes that triumphantly announce 'Only 30 minutes to cook!' must be written by people who have never had to cook while a toddler is howling from the unbearable pain in his empty stomach. I need suppers which can be prepared and cooked in something closer to five minutes! Alternatively, cooking batches of your child's favourite bolognese sauce or casserole in advance and freezing it in separate little pots will mean a supply of instant meals which only need to be defrosted and cooked.

When it comes to vegetables, parboiling fits the bill. Many vegetables, like courgettes and asparagus, cook rapidly in boiling water, which causes little loss of nutrients and keeps the crispness that can be achieved with steaming. Try boiling courgettes and asparagus in a little water in a deep skillet for no more than three minutes. If you want to avoid cleaning a pan, set your mini-potatoes to boiling and throw in your green vegetable for the last two minutes.

Cooking for yourself

Isn't it amazing the effort we are willing to put into cooking for our husbands and children while, left to our own devices, we eat crisps straight out of the bag while standing over the sink? There is no reason, really, why cooking properly for yourself cannot be healthy and easy. You have a lot of work to do, so it is worth giving yourself a decent meal or two.

If you do not have a child old enough to cultivate into a future chef or a husband who loves cooking, you will unfortunately have to cook for yourself. To feed myself during the day, I make sure I have sufficient food to cover breakfast and lunch for the week. I only do menus for dinner. In feeding yourself, using the same food items used in the baby's lunch will make sure you are eating a nutritious meal, and one that will probably fill you up. My typical lunch might be one open-faced grilled cheese sandwich with sliced tomatoes, a piece of fruit and a bowl of soup – the yummiest I can find in the supermarket deli section. I strongly recommend you eat healthy foods because a housewife, being a leader, has a lot of things to do. It isn't as if we are going to watch telly all day. The sooner you get some filling food down, the sooner you can start enjoying your afternoon doing the fun part of a housewife's job!

Hired help

If you are fortunate enough to be able to employ domestic help, your problem may be different. You may find you have too much time on your hands; that being a housewife is deathly dull. You will be reading the above thinking 'Why do I want more free time? I can't even fill the time I have now!' If I may, I would like to make a radical suggestion. Sack one of your helpers.

I know one housewife who can afford to employ a nanny, a housekeeper and a cook. You would think she would be happy, having so many people helping her with the nasty work around the house. The truth is, she is bored to tears. If you ask her how she spends her day, she cannot tell you. She takes walks with the baby, maybe visits a friend, goes to the gym and does some shopping. It sounds like a lovely life of leisure, I know, but pretty unmemorable. Without a purpose to your day, week or life, why bother getting out of bed? By employing all these people, she has made herself redundant. This is a major reason why so many high-earning families have two breadwinners. It is not financial necessity. It becomes an intellectual and spiritual necessity.

Leisure can be a burden for the human species, with our complex brains. We can savour a series of days of lying on our backs, watching the clouds pass overhead, but not a lifetime. We are not like a domestic cat who seems only to need his mistress' armchair next to a sunny window and two rich meals a day to achieve everlasting contentment.

Rightly or wrongly, humans are determined to find their purpose. Leisure is not a purpose. It is not even a worthy goal. Yet much of our working life is aimed at achieving a permanent state of leisure. We work to have enough money to go on holiday or even retire early. Wouldn't it be better if your life's work was so satisfying that you felt no need to escape?

I personally find that I love my free time because it is just fleeting enough. I don't have to wait all week or save all year in order to pursue my interests. If curiosity about anything arises in the morning, I can usually indulge myself in the afternoon. I believe I enjoy my hobbies and interests because, while I am cleaning and cooking, I can look forward to the minute the baby goes down for a nap and I can read another chapter, refine the family webpage, or come up with another community outreach project. If I could do the things I loved for eight or more hours a day, why, that would be work! The two or three hours free that I have just for myself are enough to indulge my passions most of the time, and it is certainly more free time than I had while I was working.

If you get rid of one of your helpers, whether it is a cleaner, au pair, gardener or cook, and you find you cannot manage the work on your own, then at the very least you have learned to appreciate what your helper did. On the other hand, you may find that keeping your own garden is very enjoyable, that cleaning is not so arduous, or that the helpers to whom you paid so much money were not actually doing a very good job.

When you do decide to employ help be realistic in your expectations. If you have had to juggle kids and housework yourself, the experience will make you a better employer. You will know for a fact that cleaning the bathroom with a curious toddler and dog insisting on looking directly into the toilet is not a great situation to be in. If you don't expect yourself to be the perfect parent, cleaner and dog owner simultaneously, don't demand it of anyone you employ to help you out.

Hired help does not have to be expensive, especially as the amount of help you need may be less than you think. You left work because you were not enjoying being away from your children or were too worn out to appreciate your home. Do you really want to hand your children over to a nanny all day, every day? Assess whether you want time to have coffee with a friend twice a week, or whether you need 15 hours of undisturbed time to work on your art or to study. It may be you just need a cleaner once a week or a babysitter for a few afternoons. Even someone on the tightest budget can often hire a helping hand for a few hours a week or once a month.

I know one housewife who swears by advertising for an 'errand runner' at the local secondary schools. If a teenager is organised enough to call you about the job, they are reliable enough to do a bit of garden work, dog walking or ironing, depending on their talents. She has done this for years and says she has not had a bad 'un yet. If you can fill that time with something that really engages your mind, it is money well spent.

Now that the unpleasant 20 per cent part of your job is finished, you have the rest of the day to begin doing the fun part of caring for a family and looking after yourself.

5
The heart of the matter: family

With the nitty-gritty out of the way, we can start working on the more satisfying aspects of being a housewife. Here is where the titles 'wife', 'homemaker' and 'mother' start to take on true richness of meaning.

Notice that I placed the role of wife ahead of the other roles. Mothering, or tending to our children, is almost instinctive and this role quickly leaps to the fore at any provocation. Homemaking often gets lumped in with cleaning, a topic which already causes anxiety attacks in most women. Being a wife, however, is fundamental to your new role at home. I use the terms 'husband' and 'wife' loosely, by the way, as whether you are married to your partner or not does not change the importance of your relationship to each other.

By attending to your relationship with your husband first, you can more easily create a loving, relaxed and secure environment for your children, critical for both your roles as mother and homemaker. Research conducted by Stewart Friedman at the Wharton School of Business at the University of Pennsylvania shows that both mothers and fathers are more confident as parents when they feel content in their marital, working and social spheres. This means that sacrificing yourself for your children will not make your children happy. In fact, Friedman has shown that both mothers and fathers who feel insecure in any way, either at work or at home, have children with a higher incidence of behavioural problems, ranging from whingeing to tantrums to criminal behaviour.

You and your husband need to recognise how much you need and can help each other. By improving the relationship with your spouse, you can dramatically improve your abilities as a parent and, as a result, your relationship with your children. You improve your relationship with your husband by giving just a little consideration to your role as a wife.

Being a wife means nurturing your husband

There is a movement in California called 'Surrendering'. This ultra-conservative philosophy claims that women should resign all the trappings of responsibility and intelligence and let their husbands decide everything. Surrendered wives advocate wearing frilly night things, and if a husband demands sex then the answer is always yes. Surrendered wives report that their relationships with their husbands have vastly improved.

Frankly, I think my husband would leave me if I lost my ability to make decisions about anything. He did not marry me because of my frilly night things, though they may have helped catch his attention. Most men marry intelligent, capable women because we bring out the best in our husbands. Intelligent wives are good conversationalists and reaffirm for husbands their own intelligence. What could be sexier than a smart woman who finds you attractive?

What surrendered wives have done, though, by giving up responsibility is demonstrate to their husbands that they trust them totally. Nagging is not trusting. If you trusted someone to do something, you would not ask 500 times if they had done it yet. If you can work on letting your husband know that you trust him to do the right thing, he will in turn trust you to be the best you can be in your role at home.

A husband who does not trust his wife will look for tangible proof that she is working as hard as he is. This is where the trap of striving for a spotless house and perfect kids comes in. Both are virtually impossible to achieve and easily discounted by a discontented spouse anyway.

When trust is absent, you get into the familiar 'you do not appreciate how hard I work' exchange. The problem with these arguments is they turn into an itemised list of daily hardships. While you may feel in the heat of an argument that you are giving evidence of how difficult your job is, you are also doing something very unkind. You are subtly telling your husband that you are unhappy with your life. Husbands feel responsible for the happiness of their wives, but the reality is that your happiness is largely down to you.

You are also, in a bid to convince your husband, convincing yourself that you are living a hard-knock life. The more frequently you tick off your list of grievances the more you think it is true. Provided you are not being psychologically or physically abused by your husband, your unhappiness probably has little to do with him. If your husband is at work all day, you cannot be entirely responsible for how his workday goes. The same applies to you. So instead of complaining to the man who can do little to shape your day, come up with your own programme to take responsibility for your happiness. As you do this, you may find that you can start fostering your husband's trust in you. If you have not got trust in your relationship now, building that bridge could be the most important project you have to tackle.

Husbands get frightened too

The day you decide to leave work is actually a major test of your husband's trust in you. Having devoted the whole first chapter to the fears women face in giving up their career, it would be easy to think that men by comparison do not have any problems during such a transition. They are just falling into traditional gender roles, after all. How could they be stressed?

When I left my job, even though we had discussed all my options, I had not fully appreciated how my decision would affect my husband. Men often feel neglected or unrewarded when their wives first leave work. Confronted with a wife who wants to give up work, husbands can feel torn between wanting to support their wife's wishes, while also being scared to death about the financial implications.

Husbands, by and large, want their wives to be happy. Men usually want a quiet life and they often see a happy wife as the key to domestic peace. A happy family also represents success. This is why men can feel conflicting emotions about their partner giving up work. Two incomes ensure financial security, or at least material possessions and social status. The family would have to be happy, wouldn't it?

A man may have, up to now, taken great satisfaction in seeing the family income rise steadily every year. Now, his wife shows signs of not sharing this satisfaction. If the wife and children are clearly unhappy about mum working, it would be politically incorrect to stand in the way of a good woman making a decision about how she spends her life. But a wife's decisions affect the husband's life. Indeed, the husband may feel that the wife, in spite of wanting to discuss the matter with him endlessly, will come to her own conclusions without him. He may suddenly feel out of control of his own life.

Even more worrying, these discussions may strike him as bizarre, with the wife announcing a new resolution every week about how she intends to solve her dissatisfaction. The husband, who cannot relate to this process of thinking out loud, starts working out a coping strategy for dealing with the most recent of his wife's decisions and then seven days later finds she has shot off in another direction. My husband summarised my prevarications this way:

- I would never quit work, and the children would go to a daycare centre near my office.
- Taking the children on the train for the morning commute was a dreadful idea, so we would hire a nanny.
- We don't want anyone living in our house, so we need to find a childminder instead.
- How could I employ someone on low pay to work longer hours than I was working? Plus, it couldn't be a good thing to just park my children somewhere for over 12 hours a day. We would have to change our schedules to allow both the children and the child-minder a more reasonable day.
- Alternating our schedules would not work if we had to work late or travel. Plus we would never get to see each other, let alone the children. Maybe there is more to life than working all the time.

Oh, no. I had reached the scariest conclusion of all!

With me not working at all, my husband now felt wholly responsible for the family's well-being. He believed that he absolutely could not lose his job, so he could not afford to be cavalier in his relationships at work. Business obligations took on a much greater significance. He suddenly found it much harder to say no to his superiors if they demanded his attention after hours or on the weekends.

The decision to leave work can also come during an emotionally or financially tumultuous time. Maybe the wife is expecting a child and in the throws of pregnancy-induced madness. This means when she wants to solve this work versus home problem, she wants to solve it right now! No husband would risk brushing off a pregnant woman with 'We'll discuss it when you aren't insane'. That wouldn't result in a quiet life.

You may be about to buy a house, a decision in itself which may have taken a year to make already, or you may have recently exhausted your credit card limit furnishing the nursery. Imagine the panic this could cause a husband!

If your husband has generously rolled over to your plans to stop working, be sure you let him know that you appreciate that he has given you a very precious gift. Just because you have worked and you know, maybe, that much of the workday is spent in creative procrastination, do not misunderstand your partner's apparent resentment that you now seem to have an easy life. The decision has probably been as stressful for him as it has been for you. Men like to be the good guys, so be sure to let him know, and often, what a hero he is to you and his children. After all, he has trusted you to make the right decision not only for yourself but also for the whole family. He deserves a little appreciation for that, at least.

Trust and dependence

One interesting thing that happens when a wife gives up working is a realisation by both partners of how dependent they are on each other. On top of the litany of financial and emotional fears a couple already have to face, mutual dependence can be a terribly frightening discovery.

I cannot tell you how much more I worry about my husband's safety now that I am at home. This is not because I have nothing to occupy my mind except morbid fears of death. It is because the vulnerability of me and the children is so much more obvious. Because it seems to be an irrational fear, too, partners often will not discuss what could happen if one of them is injured or killed.

The first time I mentioned this fear to my husband he said that his worry was not what happened if he died, but what he would do if something happened to me. We had never discussed what such an event meant on an emotional level before. It is not a topic you can easily bring up on a Friday evening, after all.

You as an at-home wife are not necessarily more vulnerable than your husband. He depends on you totally to stay on top of the needs of the children and the house, and though he may never have said so, this dependence may just scare him to death. It would be kind for you to one day show him that you have thought about this vulnerability and would like to teach him a little about nutrition or how the car seat works, if these are his weak spots. Ask, too, for help in planning for his death, like who to call at his work, or for legal help. Such a discussion can not only relieve quite a lot of tension, but also allow for a clear demonstration of your love and concern for each other.

Moving from fear to mutual support

The best way to help alleviate the feelings of isolation and lack of control your husband may be experiencing is to encourage him to be involved in child rearing and housekeeping. Some women feel that husbands do not appreciate how much they do around the house. Men, however, may not want to face all the work their wives do exactly because it would force a realisation of how dependent they are upon their wives, which, as we have already discussed, may be too scary for some husbands to contemplate.

Rather than asking (or nagging) for help, then, getting husbands involved in housework and childcare may be better framed as survival training. If you are going to try this approach, however, always remember that men are programmed to be problem-solvers and like to be heroes. At the same time, they may be sensitive to the fact that they do not feel as competent as you in either the parenting or cleaning department.

Research has shown that men compare their efforts around the house to their wife's ability, not necessarily to the skills of other husbands. Therefore, if there is any risk of criticism or failure in the face of such stiff competition, they may choose not to help at all. This means that you must fall back on the tools of trust and try very hard not to nag, give helpful suggestions or complain about the job they do. This is very, very hard, I know, but you are a leader and you can do it.

Getting Dad to look after the kids

Fathers can easily feel incompetent around their own children only because these little people change so quickly. Help your husband stay up-to-date with his kids and encourage him to spend time with them without you around. This way their relationship can develop unique roots, not dependent upon Mum's assumptions about either her husband's or her children's capabilities and interests.

If you have very young children and your partner's work means he does not get to see them much, don't be surprised if at first Dad does not know how to play with the kids when the weekend rolls around. Social interaction is a two-way street. It is just as likely that the children do not know how to play with Dad either.

My husband had a heart-breaking experience when our daughter was going through stranger anxiety. I had kept her up on a Friday night as usual so that Dad could bath her and put her to bed. This particular evening, when he walked in the door and expected his usually smiling, wiggling toddler to be glad to see him, she instead burst into furious tears and desperately grabbed for me.

Can you imagine a father's sadness at this greeting? Maybe you as a working mother have seen your own child treat you as a stranger. I know one hard-working mum whose child used to wake crying in the middle of the night, but not recognise his Mummy when she tried to comfort him. Fathers experience this sense of rejection frequently, often coming home to a chilly reception.

Children do not just change emotionally and socially. Childcare chores change too as the children get older, and working dads do not get to see the evolution in their children's lives the way mums at home do. My husband had been bathing the baby on his own months after she had been able to sit up and wriggle around. Unknown to me, however, he had continued to wash her hair by holding her backwards over the bathtub, like he did when she was a newborn baby, and he couldn't understand why she screamed so much!

'You never told me!' he accused, when I showed him that it was okay to use the shower. Dads are often left in the dust when it comes to childcare chores, picking up that something new has happened long after a change has come and ceased to be novel. Forgive your partner for not knowing his children as well as you do. It is not his fault. Assure him that if he hasn't helped much before, looking after the kids gets more fun the more he does it. You do not have to share the fact that it will not get any easier. No point putting him off, right?

Getting husbands to help around the house

Women who feel that their husbands are not helping enough with the housework believe, basically, that the workload is unfair. This does not necessarily mean that we expect the work to be equally divided.

Men, speaking man language, do not understand this. Men think when women say something is not fair that we want it to be equal. But equal may be impossible. Maybe you do not want your husband even to look at the laundry because he will turn it all pink. So your husband is stuck on the word equal while thinking, 'She wants me to do more, but not this, this or this because I will mess it up'. Men, caught in this brain loop, think that we are just hysterical and totally illogical so they do not change their behaviour no matter how much or how loudly we complain.

If you can accept that men speak a different language from us, you can see that what men need is a demonstration of what we really mean by the word fair.

Why can't men see the work that needs to be done around the house? Unfortunately, men do not know like women do all the details that constitute housekeeping. You will still have to provide him with a to-do list, but to provide him with some insight as to how long *your* list is you can use an exercise developed by sociologist Scott Coltrane at the University of California, Riverside.

On index cards write down housekeeping or childcare tasks, one task per card. Include traditionally 'male' chores as well, like mowing the lawn or washing the car. Monitor what you do for a week to make sure you get all the little details, like chopping vegetables, making the children's packed lunches and so forth. To get you started, here is Coltrane's list of tasks used in his study. I have added a few chores of my own and likewise feel free to add others that apply to your family.

Domestic task list

Housework
Vacuum
Mop up
Sweep
Dust
Clean sinks
Clean toilets
Clean baths and showers
Make beds
Pick up toys
Tidy lounge
Hang up clothes
Spring clean
Sweep path
Wash windows
Take out rubbish

Meal preparation and clean-up
Plan menus
Prepare breakfast
Prepare lunch
Cook supper
Make snacks
Put food away
Bake
Wash dishes
Put dishes away
Wipe kitchen worktops
Shop for groceries

Clothes care
Laundry
Hand washing
Shoe care
Sewing and mending
Buying clothes
Ironing

Home maintenance and repairs
Redecorate
General gardening
Water lawn
Mow lawn
Weeding
Interior painting
Exterior painting
Clean gutters
House repairs
Car maintenance
Car repairs
Wash car

Finances and home management
Run errands
Pay bills
Prepare income tax forms
Make investments
Handle insurance
Decide major purchases
Plan dates with partner
Book travel and holidays
Correspond with relatives/friends

Childcare
Put children to bed
Awaken children
Dress children
Bath children
Drive children
Take child to doctor
Care for sick child
Arrange babysitting
Supervise children
Discipline children
Play with children
Plan outings with children
Purchase and wrap party presents

Pet care
Walk dog
Feed animals
Take animals to vet
Administer medication to animals
Groom animals
Clean toilet mess
Obedience training
Play with animals
Clean pets' bedding
Bath animals

Source: *Family Man: Fatherhood, housework and gender equity*, Scott Coltrane, Oxford University Press (1996).

Make two sets of these cards, one for you and one for your husband. Then, sitting separately, each of you sort the cards into 'Wife's', 'Husband's' and 'Shared' piles. The chances are that your 'Wife's' pile will be much bigger than his 'Husband's' pile. Also, the chances are that his 'Shared' pile will be bigger than your 'Shared' pile.

Why this is has to do with perceptions, and it gets back to the use of language in what men and women mean by the term 'shared'. Because you speak different languages, do not immediately launch into an argument, pointing to how high the 'Wife's' job pile is as proof of how overworked you are. Just keep quiet and let your husband eye up the height of your 'Wife's' pile. Most husbands will be impressed and admit, 'Wow, it really is unfair'.

Don't use this opportunity to gloat in victory. You haven't won yet. Go through your 'Wife's' pile and pull out the tasks you want to be either shared or, better yet, turned into 'Husband's' tasks. Your husband may think a task is already shared, in which case just explain that as long as he is at home, you want him to consider it completely his job. Do not argue about what 'shared' really means, just get it out of your 'Wife's' pile!

Now that you've done all this, your husband has a new allocation of household tasks, which is still smaller than the 'Wife's' pile by the way. With great satisfaction and a generous smile proclaim to him 'Now *that* is fair!'

Your husband will be so relieved finally to understand you. He has his to-do list sorted and your understanding of fairness has been made absolutely clear to him for the first time in his life. And because you are working on trust, remember, promise that you are not going to remind him, not even once, of his jobs. You, in your wisdom, because you are a leader, trust him to carry out his defined fair share of the work.

Respect each other

The final element of trust between partners, which is often the first to be disregarded over time, is the practice of respect. Treating one another with respect, courtesy and good manners can diffuse a lot of arguments. As a leader you are entitled to be treated with respect and you are fully entitled to ask for it. Most working women do not have a problem demanding common courtesy, but it is easy to let the habit slip.

If you have begun extending demonstrations of courtesy to your husband in your bid to build trust, you are within your rights to ask that he do the same for you. Explain that just as he likes to be thanked for doing things around the house, you'd like to know that he notices you have made an effort to create a nice home. Turn your contest of who is more miserable into an exchange of complements and thank-yous.

If your husband doesn't have a great track record of noticing his surroundings, suggest to him that he makes a point of looking for something kind to say to you when he walks in the door, like, 'Wow! The house smells nice and clean,' or, 'Thanks for ironing all my shirts'.

This is your clue to say something nice back, or fill him in on some good news about the kids. Alternatively, you could try showing that you recognise he's been at work, saying, 'Boy, you look tired. I bet it's nice to be home'. Evenings can be the most fraught, since you are both tired. Starting out on a positive note will let you both start to relax, and possibly even enjoy each other's company.

Once you have built up your husband's loving support, you don't have to spend your valuable time and energy justifying your position at home. Good thing too, because your other two working roles as homemaker and mother can be a lot of fun. Devoting your attention to these areas will create family memories and bind you together. Believe me, your children will not remember how you vacuumed and dusted (Did Mum lift the ornaments off the shelf? Did she move the sofa to get under and behind it?).

Tradition, warmth and regularity of schedules and seasons will linger longest in their minds. Try this test yourself: which brings back happy associations? Wandering around a toy shop or jumping in a pile of raked leaves? Going to Disneyland with the whole family or fishing with Dad? Eating mother's carefully prepared suppers or baking cookies together after school? As an adult, can you work out which activities are more likely to create stress, possibly ruining the loving atmosphere you intended? I recommend that you minimise your physical effort, while encouraging the greatest creative effort out of you and your family.

Your home, however, is the backdrop to your family's life. The more useful you can make it, the more rewarding your creative excursions as a family will be. Turning a house into a home, though, is a lot of fun and it doesn't have to cost anything.

Being a homemaker means nurturing your home

A house that is loved has a life of its own because it is reflecting the life of its occupants. You will love your house when it can be used and properly lived in by you. I love reading design books and looking at what other people have done with colour and fabrics. However, the experts all say that style comes from the individual. You can't study it and you can't buy it. Furthermore, your whole family uses your house so your style will be invaded by the needs and tastes of others. So what you need is a family style.

For years I had read that 'style comes from within'. Lots of stuff comes from 'within', though, like happiness, confidence and peace of mind. Goodness knows we struggle to get happiness or confidence our whole lives. Does that mean it will take 40 years to discover our own style?

Fortunately, no. You do not have to analyse your past or reconcile unhappy relationships to find your style. All you need to do to get started is to take a tour of your house, either in your mind or by literally walking through it. How do people use various rooms? If they are unused, how would you like the rooms to be lived in? For example, we have banished the television from our living room, so I thought about how I would like to see people using the room instead. Obviously it would be nice to entertain in this room, have cocktails or tea. We also, during the holidays, usually put on a theatrical production in the lounge.

For everyday use, however, we love to read and the living room would be one wonderful place to do that. My husband likes to read his spy novels while I like to read decorating books and magazines, but we also enjoy spending Sundays reading the papers and drinking coffee. Finally, I would like to see the family gather in this room to play games.

Consolidating these thoughts helped me visualise the furniture and arrangement. Our family needs flexible furniture that can work in both a formal and informal context. The room would require comfortable chairs or sofas for at least two readers, tables for cups of coffee and lights that can be aimed over a reader's shoulder or act as a spotlight for a young performer. Finally, we need a low bookcase for the types of books, projects and games we like in this room. That is all we need. Anything else is clutter and may be better used in another room.

After furnishing the room according to this plan, we use the room and see if anything else is needed. We have found, over several months, that the armchairs would benefit from footstools, as we like to read in those chairs. Also I have not been happy about draping blankets on the sofa, which we have used for snuggling during cold evenings. So, I am keeping an eye out for a good blanket box or chest. Keeping the use of the room specific and comfortable allows us to buy what is really needed, not what is merely fashionable or only aesthetic.

Doing this room by room has helped crystallise each room's purpose as it fits our family. For example, I read all over the house, but I read different things in different rooms. I read parenting books in bed, while I do research or manage the family finances in the office. I like to read inspirational books while taking a bath, but I look at and assemble the family photo albums in the living room. Naturally, I read my cookbooks in the kitchen, but I like my gardening books at hand there too, since I can dash outside if I'm struck with inspiration (or dash inside if faced with a problem). With this in mind, having one room devoted to a library does not make sense since I will be dragging and leaving books all over the house. This does not make tidying up easy either. As a result, we have one or two shelves for books in nearly every room in the house. This has dramatically reduced the piles of books I used to have scattered throughout the house.

It may seem obvious that each room has a purpose, but traditional furnishing of rooms can make them non-functional for a family. If you believe living rooms are only for entertaining, you buy furniture that cannot be used except in a formal context, leaving the room uninhabited – and unloved – for 95 per cent of the year. For families who love books as we do, it's easy to think that a library is the perfect solution, when spreading bookshelves around the house according to topic may be much more useful, and result in a system which is easier to maintain and keep tidy.

Furthermore, families end up with junk rooms because they haven't designated a space for this so-called junk. It ended up in the junk room because you actually need this stuff. If it were really junk you would have got rid of it in the last jumble sale. Sort through your junk room, decide where these possessions can be better stored and reclaim this very useful space for your family to live in.

Kitchens are a special problem as well. The current belief by designers that the kitchen is where the family gathers and so must serve multiple purposes is in my opinion the result of the house not being used properly. I do not want my children playing in the kitchen. It's not safe and it is difficult enough keeping the kitchen clean and hygienic as it is without the whole family conducting all their business in there while I am trying to cook. So we have banished chairs and tables from the kitchen. If my husband would let me, the answering machine would go as well.

Take a tour through your house. Look at the possessions that have drifted into the various rooms. Maybe someone hasn't left their things behind, but has left them there because it is the room where they really belong. Imagine what activities you would like to see taking place in different rooms. Then move your furniture around to suit your family's needs. I suspect you will begin to feel more comfortable in your home and so will your family. You didn't even need to buy anything new!

Colour is another aspect of using your home that people do not often think about. The analysis many women make when picking colours depends on how much sunlight the room receives. Sunny rooms benefit usually from being cooled down with greens, blues and whites while north-facing rooms generally get dressed in warm pinks, yellows or browns.

Colour, however, has a deep psychological impact. Studies have shown that the colour of all your surroundings can influence your mood, right down to the colour paper you have in your notepad. Psychologist Dr Robert Epstein, in his *Big Book of Stress Relief Games*, suggests analysing the colour spectrum and rearranging the colours according to the level of stress or relaxation they induce in you. You can collect colour sample cards from paint manufacturers for this exercise to play with various shades of colour as well. Generally speaking, cool colours are found to be calming while hotter colours can make you feel energised or even stressed.

After I had done this exercise, I began to realise that I was attracted to doing certain activities in specific rooms not only because of their functionality, but also because of their colour schemes. For example, our bedroom is north-facing, but I decided to decorate this room in sage green and white, both cool and relaxing colours. My office, however, which is very sunny, and what I call my 'Girlie room' is decorated in lavender, purple, terracotta pink and off-white. These are quite energising, even stressful colours. When I am ready to work, my office energises me, but if I want to read, reflect or just space out I often find myself in the reading corner of my bedroom. Colour, then, exerts quite a strong influence over how I am psychologically able to use various rooms.

Try shifting the way you look at the colour schemes in your house away from what the stylistic mood is, to what the room makes you want to do, such as relax quietly, play games, study or work. Epstein notes that colours do not necessarily make you more efficient. A red kitchen won't make you wash dishes more quickly than a blue kitchen would. Rather, the colour can influence whether or not you are happy to be there.

Comfort, function and mood are just a minor part of uncovering style, however. If you use your house to reflect your values, style will begin to shine through. Think about what your family values, such as travel, food, music, history, technology, sport, gardening, animals or any other number of interests which require an investment of passion and time. If you do not love to travel but choose an African theme for a room because you found a bunch of knick-knacks on sale you probably won't love the look for long. If you don't spend much time in the country but jump on the country cottage trend, you may find the room dates itself quickly. Let your passions be your guide, and you will find a family style emerging that will withstand the test of time.

When shopping for accessories don't be motivated by an empty space on a mantlepiece. Buy something because you love it. The test is, if you can go home without buying the item and you are still thinking about it 24 hours later, you love it. Go back and buy it. If you are at a one-day craft fair, walk around the entire show, look at everything, even the things that will probably hold no interest. What you are doing is filling your mind with ideas. When you have wrapped your mind around the hundreds of things you could buy, the item you truly love will stand out. Buy it just before you leave the fair.

Often I have found at such fairs that what I loved at first sight pales in comparison to another treasure found at a later stall. Or, indeed, I forget all about my first discovery by the time I sit down for tea. If I can't remember even seeing something truly special a mere half an hour afterwards, then buying it would have been a waste of money.

The love test works at home, too. When you decide to clean out your cupboards, assess each item honestly, asking yourself, 'Do I love this?' Any answer other than 'Yes' is a 'No'! 'Sort of' does not count. If you find something and exclaim, 'so that's where it's been', and it has been missing for about five years, you obviously do not need it and you very probably do not love it. If you do love it, get it out of the cupboard and on display. Things you love reflect that love into the world, so why not put it where everyone can see it?

A major exception to this rule would be if you are still in your child-bearing years. A pregnancy can come unannounced and I would never advise a woman to get rid of her fat clothes, no matter how much she may hate them. There is nothing so discouraging as getting out of hospital with a newborn baby and not having anything to wear but maternity clothes. Stash your fat wardrobe (if you're not wearing it at the moment, that is) in the loft or at your mother's with your maternity clothes. You don't need it to be instantly handy.

Having a home that reflects the passions of your family will make it feel loved by all who cross its threshold. Organising rooms by the way your family uses them will lessen the time it takes to tidy up, and shopping for your home using the love test will help minimise the clutter that needs cleaning. Following these basic guidelines, a family style should emerge, and your home will begin to exude comfort without spending much money at all.

To make sure your house evolves as your family needs change, potter. Children grow quickly, so this is a good reason to potter a lot.

Pottering generally starts with some apparently, to the untrained eye, pointless wandering around your house or garden, looking at your stuff. Humming is a good dramatic touch to pottering, but people may worry if 'The Wheels on the Bus' is what is quietly coming out of your mouth.

As you dawdle in a room, take note of what happens to catch your attention. Suddenly, a thought will flash across your brain: 'I hate that vase' or 'That toy cupboard is not childsafe'.

This is what you are looking for: clues as to how your tastes and the needs of your family are changing. Through pottering, your brain is given a chance to reassemble millions of pieces of information about your possessions and your schedule that, in the middle of it all, you ordinarily cannot process in a logical way.

By pottering around your house, staring at your belongings, musing at photos, and generally day-dreaming, your family's life will suddenly come together in your mind. You will see the light coming through a certain window, and the fact that all your children are walking and not putting things in their mouths means you can have a potted rubber tree plant just like you always wanted, but had forgotten until now. Maybe a magazine lying open on a certain coloured page will contrast just perfectly with your duvet cover, and as luck would have it you have got accessories in that colour scattered willy-nilly around the house.

Pottering is a lot of fun, takes little time, usually costs nothing, and can improve the way you use your house. In spite of appearances, pottering is actually a critical creative skill that can be applied to an infinite variety of problems and projects. Most people find pottering in their house quite easy. Later, you will see how pottering can unleash both your talents and your untapped intelligence.

Being a mother means nurturing your children

Mothering is not just about keeping your child fed, clothed and safe. If it were, all children could just be institutionalised and raised by experts 24 hours a day. Parenting, most people would agree, also means imparting a bit of yourself, your family history and your values to your child. This truly valuable aspect of parenting is carried out through both playing with and educating your children.

Playtime

One of the most fun jobs that a housewife takes on is playing with her children. Play, in fact, is an important part of the social dynamic of any family, not just human families, as it teaches the young of any species rudimentary social and survival skills. Play is also psychologically vital, helping to form emotional bonds between parent and child as well as between siblings. Even if your children are older, it is still crucial that you interact with them as much as possible. Not only is it good for the parent-child relationship, but it is very important for children's brain development up until the onset of puberty to experience frequent and genuine expressions of affection.

This is one reason why over-scheduling your child's day with too many classes and activities is not a great idea. A child's sense of security comes from her understanding of her role within the family. If you don't allow family relationships time and freedom to develop, your child may find it harder to ward off the effects of stress as she grows to adulthood. The reason is because friendships are inherently less intimate and more transient than family relationships. As such, a child's experience of love will be limited if she spends most of her playtime away from parents and siblings.

Recent research suggests that touching, in particular, is health promoting, as it stimulates serotonin production in the brain. Serotonin blocks the destructive effects of stress on brain cells, meaning that a child who has been lovingly handled will weather the stresses of life better than a child who has not felt the expression of his parents' love.

One game I play with my baby is One Hundred Kisses. Parents are often encouraged to hug and kiss their children every day. I say, kiss them one hundred times a day! When I get tired, then the stuffed animals take over kissing. Even the washcloth gets its kisses in, especially behind the ears.

Playtime is not just for showing your love. It is a great opportunity to teach your child about the world. For example, when playing with babies, keep in mind that their job at this stage in life is to explore their world. So pulling them away from the mobile phone and handing them a rubber teething ring is not a very stimulating exchange from a baby's point of view. I have found it much more rewarding to let her play with the telephone or cooking utensils if she wants to. She wants to play with the same things she sees the adults 'playing' with. Over time, most of the household objects lose their appeal as their mystery fades.

With this in mind, when you do buy toys for your children look for ones that you yourself would enjoy playing with, like bricks or toy cars. When your baby sees that these fascinate you, they will also fascinate her, whether you are playing with them at the time or not. Do not, however, be tempted to show small children how to play with these toys. Babies already know adults are clever, and their parents especially so. Seeing you stack bricks 15 high when they can only balance three may actually discourage them from trying. If your baby joins you in playing with the bricks, let her take over or show you what the game is going to be.

As children get older, their brains begin to function more and more like adults' brains. This means they can fall into lazy thinking patterns, especially if they attend school and adults have very conveniently scheduled events into every minute of the day. Later in the book we will look at a number of creativity games you can play with your children which over time should help them, and you, become more adept at finding and pursuing personal interests without relying too much on outside help. The goal is to prevent you turning into the resident entertainment director. After all, playing with your children does not have to take up all your time.

Staying out of the way

Everyone needs time alone, to think things over or just laze around. Kids do too. One housewife I know said the best advice she ever received was from her mother-in-law, who told her to put the kids in their rooms to play by themselves for one hour every day. Children, even babies, need this time to work on crawling, a new word, a fun pretend scenario, skimming stones or whatever it is kids do on their own. It is much harder to do this with a parent dancing around in front of them all the time. Kids are very imaginative. They really don't need much help. And an adult getting involved can actually inhibit imaginative play.

John Holt, a long-time proponent of education reform, describes in his book, *How Children Learn*, how distressing it is to see a teacher pull out a guitar, play some music and then call out 'Pretend you are a snowflake!' The children dutifully prance around, waving their hands in the air. But children left on their own to play would never shout out 'I know! Let's be snowflakes!' Holt, agreeing with other child psychologists, believes that children need pretend play to help them get to grips with real life. Thus they play 'house', 'hospital' or 'school'. Even when they play 'Superman' or 'cowboys and indians', their fantasy games involve social relationships and have a basis in reality, whether it concerns work, family or chasing criminals. Adults, in contrast, use fantasy as an escape from real life, and thus think 'snowflakes' would be an enjoyable game, while to a child it is probably meaningless.

Adults tend to look for projects and activities with the end result in mind: what do they learn, where will I get, what will I see? Children focus more on the process: colouring, hopping on one leg or running just to run. So when you play with your children, let the games be invented by your child most of the time. You will lower the incidence of frustration for you both dramatically.

Stepping back from your child does not mean you both disappear into different rooms. You can stay involved in your child's play, but not interfere with her experiments, by simply observing and listening to your child rather than worrying about entertaining her all the time. This can enrich your experience of being a parent and make you more appreciative of how unique your child truly is.

Watching my own children grow up has not only been startling, but it has made me question a lot of theories about how children learn. The experience has helped me appreciate that the accepted milestones, such as walking and speaking, are only tiny parts of a child's total development.

By becoming an audience to your child, opinions of experts and relatives who do not actually know your child can be placed into their proper context. Late-speaking children, for instance, often cause parents undue worry, when careful observation of the child over time shows that their other skills are normal or even highly advanced. Children are very complex after all, and most developmental markers are feeble indicators of whether a child is thriving socially and intellectually.

Staying at home with your children and just watching them work out how the world operates is fascinating work. If you can pull back from being an entertainer and become instead an observer of your child's emerging talents and personality, you may begin to appreciate even more deeply the miracle of human life.

Standing back from your children can also allow you to go off and do your own thing. This will not emotionally scar your children, leaving them with an abandonment complex. Studies show that a child's confidence comes from experiencing a loving and involved upbringing. This does not mean at-home mums are wonderful because they improve a child's self-esteem. Children in a good quality care environment can have the same secure experience, and thus also develop confidence.

What this does mean is if you are a housewife and have some hot personal projects that need an hour of your devoted attention which your four-year-old is not letting you have, day care will not undermine your duties as a housewife or loving mother. By taking time for yourself you will have accomplished two worthy goals: stimulating your kids and stimulating yourself. Likewise, if your toddler is driving you mad on a regular basis, and One Hundred Kisses is just not going to happen, day care does not mean you are neglecting any of your obligations. I know of housewives who think at-home mums who have help caring for the children are frauds. Ignore these people. Perhaps they have nerves of steel. Just cross these women off your list of friends. You do not need their input.

Asking for help is never wrong. In fact it is a sign of intelligence when someone demonstrates that they are aware of their limitations. If a mother needs a hand with her children, it is perfectly fine to ask for it. Refusing to recognise that you need help can in fact put your children in jeopardy if you are not careful. When I became pregnant with my second child I realised that I needed help when in the middle of the afternoon I was falling dead asleep while playing with my very awake toddler. It only had to happen once for me to know that this was dangerous, and twice for me to realise that I needed help, and fast.

Mothers who need help but feel they are the only ones capable of looking after their children are martyrs. Martyrs die painful deaths and win no awards in this life. Worse, a lot of people think martyrs are annoying. It is no fun to be a martyr, and you are not doing anyone any good by behaving like one, so go ahead and hire a babysitter.

What if you have a child with a history of behaviour problems? Will taking time out for yourself cause a child to be more disruptive? Some women stop working because they feel their children will act up less with Mum at home. I once cared for a family with three very intelligent girls. When they were with me, they were almost always on their best behaviour. As soon as their mum walked through the door, however, they became disobedient, scatter-brained and whingey. Do children only test their parents when parents do not have the time or energy to be firm?

A former nanny I know has seen this behaviour over and over with all of her families. She worried what the relationship would be like with her own children and gave up work during her pregnancy. It did not make any difference. Her child, she says, is the most challenging one she's cared for yet, even though she is at home full time.

Perhaps the need for children to test parental authority, rather than that of other carers, is part of our genetic programming. Perhaps children manipulate parents because they can see that the relationship they have with parents is fundamentally different on an emotional level, whether the parents spend the whole day with them or just a few hours before bedtime. Some children with behaviour problems may indeed benefit from mother staying home from work, but I believe the arguments about how mums spend their day as the basis for behavioural problems in children has been over-simplified and helps no one.

Some rather more interesting research into behaviour problems has suggested that, in some cases, the modern educational system might be more to blame than parents. Indeed, the idea that state schools provide a haven from broken homes and dangerous communities may in fact be false.

Education

As a parent, you have the opportunity to endow your children with a love of learning and counter-balance some of the damage to self-esteem that schools can inflict. The most radical way that you can be involved in your child's education is through home education. If this is too extreme for your tastes, home education methods can inspire fun ways for every family to incorporate play and learning together at home.

By taking control of education, you, the housewife, can really play an active role in guiding your child's life. Indeed, all at-home mothers educate at home until their children reach the age of five, but the increasing professionalisation of the education system has devalued the profoundly formative work mothers do with their young children.

Early education is not just letters, shapes and colours. Many projects you do with your child have educational value. For example, you can spend time going on field trips, while incorporating reading, writing and numeracy in more practical activities. A day's project, perhaps, may be spent in the garden. Reading might involve studying the instructions on seed packets or doing a bit of research about how to prepare a vegetable patch. Writing could be practised in keeping a gardening journal or simply writing out identifying tags for the seeds planted. Maths is covered in everything from counting out seeds or drills, to calculating the area to be planted or, with older children, mixing up fertiliser in the right quantities. Science would of course be involved in understanding what plants need to grow, why some need sun and others need shade, to carrying out and understanding soil tests. History could be learned during a trip to a nearby public garden, either concerning the estate you visit or in connection with exotic plant collections. This could inspire a geography lesson, such as why cacti or mangoes do not grow naturally in the UK. Your child does not have to be school age for a project like this. You can begin exposing children to the complexity inherent in your village from the age of two.

Gardening is only one example of how a parent can create an intellectually stimulating and challenging project for a child that also covers a wide range of educational subjects. The same can be done for many life experiences, such as visiting a friend with a newborn baby, cooking lunch, touring a wildlife rescue centre or interviewing people you meet about their jobs.

You don't need to sign up for classes to provide educational experiences. I once phoned a parent who was hosting a meeting for home-educated families. The lesson was biology and the 22 children in attendance were pond-dipping. They would drop small pails to the bottom of the pond and see first with their eyes what was brought up, then look again under a microscope. My immediate thought was 'Hey, I want to go pond-dipping!'

A younger group of home-educated children once had a meeting where they learned about different vegetables, such as what country they originally came from, some ways to prepare them and how they keep you healthy. After this discussion, the children then got to turn aubergines, leeks and shitake mushrooms into animals with the help of paper, glue, glitter and toothpicks. Such so-called 'lessons' make perfect family activities. If the children enjoy them, they can be done every weekend and cost much less than riding or dancing lessons, and can be more memorable than a trip to an amusement park.

If you have an interest in home education and live in the UK or Europe, contact Education Otherwise (see Addresses, page 187).

This organisation helps families with the logistical and legal issues involved with home education, and provides a network of families for support.

For the rest of us, there are stacks of books with suggestions for educational play, but the best way to find enjoyable projects for your family is to be inspired by your child's specific interests and talents. Coming up with activities you can both enjoy and learn from, however, requires imagination. In the next several chapters we will look at how to switch your creativity on so that you can invent fun things to do both for yourself and for your family.

6
Building a positive foundation for life

Many people who consider leaving their jobs or face retirement worry about what they will do with themselves, knocking around the house all day. Fear not. Once you learn how to switch on your creativity you will be so busy you will need to buy an organiser. For prospective new mothers, a great fear is that your mind will turn to mush. Harnessing your creativity will prevent this and possibly make your mind even more electric than when you were working. I have had times when my personal projects are so interesting, sending adrenaline zooming around my body, that I can't sleep at night for the excitement of getting up the next day and doing more.

There are plenty of housewives who are finding their time at home very stimulating and fun. Sam, for instance, has a whole list of projects that slot perfectly into the odd hour or half hour she has free. What does she do with her spare time? 'Lots of things! Play the guitar, surf the net, aerobics, swimming, dressmaking . . . I haven't really developed new interests, but I do appreciate the ones I have a lot more.'

Creativity is not just about art or crafts. It is about living your life fully, with your full attention. If you can enjoy a perfect summer afternoon, eating your lunch in the back garden, or inspecting the geraniums because you feel like looking at some terrific red blooms, then you are tapping into your creativity. If you read a newspaper with interest, debating the stories in your head, coming up with solutions or insightful opinions, you are being creative. If you walk into a shop you have never been in before and instead of shopping you think, 'Now this is a great business! I bet they make a lot of money with this concept', you are experiencing and appreciating creativity. You are living in the present and seeing your surroundings for what they are, and how they affect you and the lives of others.

When you live this way, you are motivated to capture the essence of life's experiences and share this purity with others. Thus people are motivated to create art, poetry, crafts, even businesses, seminars and websites. It isn't hard work to live in the creative state. It is fun.

Some people are lucky enough to live creatively through their work. However, many people feel that work kills creativity. Being a housewife frees you from the work environment and gives you the unusual opportunity to live a creative life.

A lot of people look around bashfully at the mention of creativity. 'I'm not artistic. I can't do anything creative.' Rubbish. Living is an act of creativity in itself. If you roll out of bed and go through the motions of your day at someone else's command, watching the clock all day, every day, because you are looking forward to watching television that evening without even knowing what is on, you are denying your creativity. You need help. You need healing. Here is what you do.

First you must turn off negativity. This is very important because nothing kills motivation faster than self-doubt stemming from fear, depression or grief. If you are in a rut, you can give yourself a good foundation for the rest of your life by doing two radical things: turn off the media and limit your friends.

Television

The first thing you must do is never watch your television again. Television numbs mind and body. If you have a baby under one year of age you can see this yourself. Put babies in front of a television and they are instantly mesmerised. They will literally not move for extended periods of time. I can see how this may be attractive if you have a rampaging four-year-old on your hands. However, for a young baby, this is unnatural and unhealthy considering that they need to be building physical strength in their limbs, working on dexterity and exercising their minds. As a parent, you probably also want them to be working on wearing themselves out so they will gratefully fall asleep the minute you snuggle them into their cot!

For adults, television has even worse knock-on effects. If no news is good news, then the evening news must by definition be pretty depressing indeed. If you want a happy life, don't watch the news. You cannot control the information flow coming out of the box and into your life. You will see death, corruption, murder and lots of politicians refusing to negotiate or be productive. You will learn little by watching the news.

I am not saying shroud yourself in ignorance. If you want to keep abreast of current events, read the newspaper. You can edit the information you take in and it sets a good example for your children. In fact reading the Sunday papers as a family can be a pleasant tradition that your children will remember fondly as adults.

Another peculiar feature of television is its remarkable convincingness. What television portrays, even when we know it is fiction, is easily accepted by the brain as fact. In 1977 the pseudonymous Jerry Mander published a book called *Four Arguments for the Elimination of Television*, which reviewed research showing that prolonged periods of inactivity can cause the brain to switch into a meditative state, making it susceptible to outside suggestion. Even though television programmes are probably not generally being used to indoctrinate the masses, we are still susceptible to accepting what we see as absolute fact. After all, we saw it with our own eyes! Many prejudices and stereotypes are formed and confirmed by what we see on television, even though they may be contradicted by our real-life experiences.

You may think is a shocking thing to say: that subconscious thought patterns can develop even though we may have actual experience to oppose these beliefs. There is research to suggest, however, that this can be the case.

Dr V S Ramachandran, professor of cognitive psychology at the University of California San Diego, works with patients who are apparently delusional about their physical abilities. His subjects are primarily stroke victims who have lost the use of a limb, but are most emphatic that they are in no way paralysed at all.

It is currently accepted in cognitive psychology that the left hemisphere of the brain is responsible for our belief system: it accepts programming of what we take to be fact, and works hard to defend this understanding of how the world works. The right hemisphere of the brain acts as a balance, questioning accepted beliefs and even proposing alternatives. This interaction of the two hemispheres is how we are able to learn new things or solve unusual problems. Faced with a dilemma, our left brain tries to find similarities to experiences we have had before. When this does not work, our right brain kicks in, forcing us to take seriously new or conflicting information.

If the right hemisphere of the brain has been damaged, as in the case of a stroke, then our left brain may not be able to accept the new and unusual information that a limb is paralysed. Faced with the fact that the limb does not move on command, the left brain begins to develop reasons, but still draws off past experience, such as the limb is weak or tired or is just moving very slowly today.

So, if you have allowed your surroundings to feed you information that society is violent, that one gender or another is stupid, or that buying stuff is fun and satisfying, it takes some effort or an overwhelming weight of evidence for even your healthy right brain to be able to reprogramme your belief system.

This may be why 'Eureka' moments, when you realise and accept a radical new idea, are so powerful. After all, something pretty major has just occurred in your brain! This also helps explain why social prejudices are so difficult to overcome, not just within society, but within ourselves. Turning off your television can stop the pattern of reinforcing false beliefs and allow you to begin gathering information for yourself about how the world works.

Television not only paints a false picture of the world around you, it can actually make you think less of yourself, by setting up false comparisons between you and the lives you see portrayed. Shows that are attractive have action, adventure, romance, beauty, travel, fabulous people, and endless products you are told you need to buy. In short you are bombarded by fictional lives full of people and events that you are not experiencing because you are camped out on a sofa for hours at a time.

Advertising then becomes particularly effective because the show already has you convinced that your life is not as interesting as the lives you are watching. Suddenly a spokesperson pops up and announces 'Your life is unfulfilling (a premise you agreed to while watching the show) . . . buy this!'

'Yes, yes, yes!' your subconscious shouts. 'Let's go shopping!'

It is a lie, and you know it. Money and possessions are very nice, but they won't bring you happiness. Buying things for your kids will not bring them happiness either. Turn your television off and you can direct all this new-found free time into making your own, very real, fabulous life.

Turning off the television amazingly does create more hours in the day, because it has a sneaky way of eating up time without your awareness. 'What do you do with your free time?' I have asked many women.

They laugh hysterically. 'What free time?' Their days are full of caring for their families. Give them a few minutes though and they will comment that they watched television for three hours last night. Forgive me for pointing this out, but watching television when you are doing nothing else means you watch television when you have free time. The problem is that no one wants to admit in public, or possibly even to themselves, that given one or three empty hours in a day they have nothing better to do than watch television.

Don't get me wrong. I have my couch potato days, when I am sick, injured or eight months' pregnant. I also get addicted to shows occasionally. But channel surfing when you are healthy but idle, let me be honest, is a waste of your life.

I recommend taking the television out of your living room. When I toured my house I didn't want the instinct of turning on the tube to override all other activities that could take place in my lounge. Put the television in another room. Make your living room a place for life. In fact, save yourself some money and cancel your cable. You will not need it anymore and in a few weeks time, I promise, you will not even miss it.

Maybe you have come to depend on television for all your entertainment. Don't worry, because everything in the programme listings has a real-life alternative.

You are probably thinking it is impossible. What about watching sport? Sport is great to watch. Enjoy it even more and watch the game at a friend's house. Even better, go and buy tickets and watch the match live. Brighten a child's day and go and cheer at school sporting events. You may see a future star player and spend a nice day outside as a bonus.

But you love the movie channels. Use your VCR. Renting videos costs less than paying for a movie channel. Plus you can watch what you want, when you want, something digital television is trying to provide at tremendous cost to you. Join an independent video shop for a more eclectic variety of films. My test of a good video shop is their selection of classic movies from the 1940s and 1950s. Even better, go to the cinema. Better still, go with friends. And finally, best of all, make your own home movies with that video camera that only gets dragged out on holiday. You will create a happy day for your family, a violence-free movie your kids will want to see again and again, and memories for your children that will last their whole lives.

But you are addicted to the soaps. Read romance novels. You can buy them cheap at second-hand book shops or borrow them for nothing from the library, and you set a good example to your children by reading (which you will probably do a lot and often, if this is your particular passion).

One of the attractions of soaps is the tension of following a long-running story. I have to tell you that life is stranger than fiction. Visit a neighbour or friend. Socialising doesn't have to be about gossip. You may find that someone you know is having relationship problems and you might just be able to help. Life itself is full of drama and eccentricity. You don't need television to find and follow a good story.

No matter how strong your TV addiction, you can be weaned in a week, guaranteed. You are stronger than television. You *can* turn it off. Once you have, you may be amazed by the richness of the world around you.

I have a dear friend who is very creative. A favourite weekend activity of hers is secretly snapping photos in the dressing rooms of designer boutiques so she can make copies of the outfits at home for herself – for fun. She also writes songs, paints, gardens, cooks and programmes computers, among dozens of other hobbies which arise as and when she is inspired.

About 10 years ago she went on a media diet: no television, radio, magazines or newspapers for a whole year. The purpose was to refresh her creativity by gathering stimulus only from the environment and people surrounding her. She did some interesting experiments in her quest to pay attention to her life. A favourite was strapping a tape recorder to her ankle for day hikes up mountains.

Back at home she would listen to these tapes like background music and the sounds would of course recall the day, but they also captured details that on her walk she may not have noticed at the time. The world is full of detail that even the most alert cannot notice and fully appreciate. So, get out of your house and experience what you have been missing!

Try turning off the television for a week. Have a plan for what you will do instead when the urge to crash out hits you. Determine what it is that television provides: humour, drama, or education, for example, and come up with your own non-TV substitute. You may want to go to the library the day before the television is switched off for good. Or, keep a list of your friends' telephone numbers handy, so that instead of zoning out you improve your social life. Do this just for yourself. You don't have to make the whole family do it, yet. You will be startled at how quickly your brain starts to splutter to life again by banishing the television. I promise.

Change your radio station

Music is great for the soul and it can be a wonderful source of inspiration. However, just as television can manipulate your mind, I believe not being selective about your radio station can damage your self-image.

As a housewife, you may already be at risk of seeing your life as dull. If you are having your first child, the lack of freedom to go out and party like you used to can be a real downer and the last thing you need is a DJ insinuating how cool everyone else in the world is. There are plenty of radio stations that do not trade on 'cool' and it doesn't mean limiting yourself to classical music or Radio Four if you are used to listening primarily to Radio One. Surf the airwaves and try a new station every day for a week. Pay attention to both the advertising and chat. Make sure that it doesn't cause you to long for a life of discos and late-night drinking because while you have young children this will probably be a rare event for you.

If you can't find a radio station you like with programming that does not depend on put-downs, sensationalism or show-off chatter, then it is time to take a look at your compact disc collection. I went on a radio strike for several years. I found out about new musicians or new albums by reading the music press and talking to my friends.

Looking for new music for your collection can be an avenue, too, for expanding your range of conversation outside of children, by the way.

Radio is often the soundtrack to our lives. Why not choose something that will boost your mood or even expand your mind?

Stop your magazine subscriptions

Magazines, too, are vehicles designed to sell you products. However, they rely on compelling articles to get you to buy the magazine. The problem is that the articles in many magazines can descend into sensationalism. If you buy magazines to have lying around for those moments when you are bored, you are doing two things: you may be denying yourself the opportunity to do something really fun or interesting and you are letting yourself be indiscriminate about what information gets logged into your mind.

Obviously, magazines are not all bad. I enjoy reading magazines as much as anyone. However, reading just anything does not set a foundation for positive thinking. I personally buy magazines one at a time, not by subscription. That way I can assess before I give away my hard-earned money whether there is anything truly worth reading. Is there an article about one of my passions or current problems? Is the article any good at addressing that issue? Sometimes the headlines sound great, but because of space constraints the article itself is so cursory it is not worth reading.

Finally, the best reason to limit the availability of magazines, especially fashion magazines, in your home is the heavy use of models in trendy clothes. If you've just had a baby, the last thing you probably need is skinny people wearing midriff-baring, bottom-hugging clothes paraded in front of you. For positive thinking, you don't need to set yourself up with unreasonable points of comparison. You can only be discouraged.

Many families use television, radio and magazines as background noise or to kill time. What they fail to appreciate is that even though they are not paying close attention to the messages being broadcast, the tone of the programming still has a powerful influence over their moods and attitudes. For this reason, making the decision to edit this media in your life instils a sense of discrimination. After all, you do not go to the theatre or to a concert indiscriminately. You pick your entertainment with the intention of enjoying it. Why not treat the media with the same critical attention?

Limit your friends

Eliminating the media's influence over your life is only half the battle against negativity. Your social network also exerts a strong influence over how you see your creative abilities. Society is full of negativity. A great way to kill inspiration is to share your ideas with cynical people. If you are early on in fostering your creativity, or are maybe feeling just a little fragile or crabby, don't share your great ideas unless you know they will be encouraged. Once you get more comfortable with your creativity you can begin discussing your projects with a broader circle of people, like your neighbours or relatives. Soon you may think of talking to agents, investors, gallery owners or store managers. With these people you must expect a high degree of rejection and criticism, so make sure you can see your projects clearly as the success they are meant to be.

People love to warn you away from doing something interesting. For every career I have ever pursued I have met five people telling me to forget it for every one who encouraged me to go for it. Writer Paul Theroux encounters this attitude all the time, every time he wants to try a difficult rowing trip or travel somewhere exotic.

In his essay 'Paddling to Plymouth', he writes, 'I suppose people say those things because they do not want to be held responsible for another person's foolishness, and because they cannot imagine anyone doing something they would not do themselves'.

Most people who tell you not even to try a venture don't speak from personal experience. When I was 20 I was foolish enough to mention to a career counsellor at university that I wanted to work for the United Nations.

'You'll never do that. There's too much competition.' Well, with over 15 million people working in New York City, any job I wanted was going to be competitive. In my experience critics just do not know what they are talking about. If you are passionate about trying something, ignore the nay-sayers. They know nothing.

Maybe you will not succeed, but by failing even to try you are missing out on an opportunity to spice up your life. Theroux comments that 'Half the thrill of it was that I had never done it before'. Why live life doing the things you have already tried? Why not try something new? It might be fun!

In spite of limiting your cynical friends, you will not find yourself alone if you stick to pursuing a creative path. Creativity is contagious. When I feel down, I call or visit one of my creative friends. They are usually working on something exciting and are always encouraging of my own ideas. Our interests and energy levels always benefit from the cross-fertilisation.

You will also find that your life starts to shine, attracting people to you and unwittingly inspiring others. When you are living creatively yourself, you will find people approaching you and telling you how you have motivated them. If that isn't rewarding, I don't know what is!

Your husband can be a wonderful friend in this way. If he doesn't start out being supportive of your ideas it is probably because he has to work long hours in an uncreative and draining environment. If you start living a more vibrant life, enriching your home, your spouse will begin to change. He will become more supportive and more creative in his own right. When I began investing creative energy in my family, I gradually saw my husband become more energised. He began calling me from work to tell me what he wanted to do in the garden. Sometimes he would come home early because he couldn't wait to get cracking on his ideas.

When you are secure in your own talents you will find the creativity of others is not threatening. You'll become more positive and encouraging and you will want to share the wonderful life you are living with your family.

However, negativity is also contagious. Surround yourself with unhappy people and you will be unhappy. We all know the saying 'misery loves company'. Well, failures love other failures, complainers love other complainers, and tired people love other tired folk. Singer Erykah Badu sings in *Apple Tree*, 'I pick my friends like I pick my fruit'. So dump your rotten friends and choose to spend time with only the bright, fresh, sweet people in the world. You may find that only your children fit into this category for a while, but over time creative people will be attracted to you by your new-found energy.

Respect your creativity

Now that you have firmed up your foundation by getting rid of the negative influences in the world that are controllable, it's time to turn on the tap and let the creativity flow!

Squeak, squeak, squeak. You may find that you twist those taps back and forth but barely a drop of an idea comes struggling out. You have got a clog. The journal page or canvas stays blank no matter how long you stare. The kids say they're bored and you can't come up with anything to do either. You wake up in the morning and cannot even face getting out of bed because it's just cleaning or bills or telephone calls.

The creative mind is just like a shy person at a party. It needs to be drawn out, encouraged with respect, happy chatter, interested questioning and attentive listening. Creativity needs a sympathetic audience and that audience is you. Not your husband, not your neighbour, kids or friends. It needs you and your respect first.

If you don't think you have any good ideas, then you have gone far down the path of disrespecting your creative abilities and you may need to start by proving you can appreciate, without envy, the creativity of others. Sara Ban Breathnach in her book *Simple Abundance* has a technique called the Discovery Journal. The Discovery Journal allows you to regress to when you were probably four years old and were finally allowed to go through and cut up your mother's magazines. I keep a large artist's sketchpad for my Discovery Journal and will occasionally flip through magazines cutting out pictures of anything capturing my fancy. The pictures or phrases can be glued into the journal randomly, as Ban Breathnach suggests, or you can group them by theme. Either method gives you a page of appealing images to meditate on whenever you need inspiration.

The Discovery Journal allows you safely and privately to examine your interests, desires and cravings. The superficial motive which inspires you to cut out that £10,000 designer dress from *Vogue* will not be the same emotion you feel once you begin to study your collection of images. The Discovery Journal has allowed you to create a symbolic picture of whom you really are. You are not an expensive dress. You are someone who loves sky blue because it reminds you of spring, someone who remembers the joy of dressing dolls in long silk scarves so that you can conjure up lengthy fairy stories. Buying the dress would not make it spring and it would not help you write a successful novel, but dreaming about the dress could take you a long way towards fostering your imagination.

Keeping a written journal is another terrific way to show your creative mind respect. Every interesting little thought that pops out, write it down. Don't judge whether something is good enough to write down. Let the creative force know that you are receptive to all new ideas and little by little your mind will become more productive and even efficient.

Writing down ideas, though, merits a warning about the limitations of language, especially if you are new to paying respect to your creative self. Language is a tool. Just as you might use a crystal to analyse the properties of light, language crystallises thought. This is useful, but has tremendous limitations. If you focus too closely on the light refracted through your crystal, say even climbing a mountain to ensure the clearest possible rays from the sun, you may miss the more spectacular display of light spread across your mountain peak and over the valleys and lakes below. The crystal will help you understand what the essence of light is, but in doing so, it has to edit out the effect of light on countless other surfaces.

The same is true with trying to get a grip on what is going on in your brain. Language allows us to give some shape to the unruly and often hazy ideas and emotions that grip the mind, but it is self-limiting. Ideas, once they are written down, can lose their power once refracted through language.

I am sure you have woken in the night with some fantastic solution to a problem, words to a presentation, or musical composition. Because we value our sleep, we just might reach over and scribble down a few notes in the dark so that we can hurriedly slip back into unconsciousness. Come morning, we can make neither head nor tail of our drowsy scrawl and the idea, or the hasty conversion of it into language, appears to be rubbish. You may find yourself saying 'This is no good'. In fact, it is not the idea that is poor, but your verbal translation of it. The Discovery Journal is useful in that it relies more on visual representation, which can be more fluid and carry more layers of meaning than words.

By pasting images down, however, you can be limiting free association. A variation on the Discovery Journal to solve this problem is a 'Paper Doll box', made up of cut-out images of your own choosing. When I was very small I loved to play with paper dolls. However, my paper dolls were not only the ones made for hanging paper clothes, with little tabs folding over their cardboard shoulders. In my Paper Doll box, I had cut-out pictures of people, babies and animals from magazines and newspapers. My characters and stories could change easily and I could add images as my mother let me cut up her magazines.

Your grown-up Paper Dolls can be played with in a similar way to stimulate creativity, one day sorted by colour or mood just for fun, or used on another day to help you solve a particular problem. Negativity comes from being stuck in a rut. In order to lift yourself up, you must expose yourself to change. You don't need to divorce your husband or move house. You could just rummage through your Paper Dolls and make some new, unexpected juxtapositions of favourite ideas.

Paper Dolls and the Discovery Journal are not just airy-fairy ways to waste time. Both these tools allow you to begin practising random association of ideas while providing you with a library of images and symbols that you personally enjoy.

In addition to learning to appreciate the creativity of others and letting their work fire your own imagination, it is well worth having a stash of compliments people have paid you. I have an artist friend who has a 'Thank You Drawer'. This small drawer in her desk holds all the thank you notes and words of congratulation she has ever received for a job well done. Whenever she is feeling untalented or incapable, she riffles through her Thank You Drawer to boost her confidence, finding proof that there are people in the world who think she's pretty talented. You do not have to depend only on yourself for pats on the back. Others have appreciated your efforts, too. Why not set up your own Thank You Drawer?

Find other ways of your own to let your creative self be expressed, acknowledged and respected by you. If you try playing a piece of music or writing a business plan, approach it with the view that this is a gift in equal parts from God and from a small child. To neither would you say 'This is no good'. Respecting its preciousness, say 'Thank you. This is wonderful'. Because it really is.

Can't you outsmart negative influences?

You may think all these techniques are ridiculous. You may be saying to yourself right now, 'I am a free-thinking, independent-minded individual. I am perfectly capable of seeing through the artifices of television, fashion magazines and critics who don't know what they are talking about. Nor am I so pathetic that I cannot associate two images or ideas just because they are on different pages'.

The human mind, however, is designed to collect facts and set up neurological shortcuts, as Dr Ramachandran has shown in his studies of the right and left brain in belief systems. However, the brain is also constantly monitoring your surroundings whether you are aware of it or not.

Dr Colin Blakemore of Oxford University has been researching a phenomenon called blind sight. This is an unusual condition where someone is by all definitions truly blind, but is still able to sense his surroundings using visual references. This happens when the information that is normally collected through the eye and processed in the visual cortex, the common understanding of sight, does not occur, but the visual cortex is stimulated via a second route through the brain stem. The brain stem is associated with reflexive behaviour, which suggests that visual data is collected not just on a conscious level, but also on an unconscious level. All healthy humans have blind sight, with the brain monitoring our surroundings for hints of unusual or dangerous activity that may be out of our immediate attention. If a tiger suddenly appeared off to your left, your blind sight would, we hope, cause you to turn your eyes to the left even though you never expected to see a tiger nearby.

This monitoring allows us to move through the world on a kind of autopilot. We do not have to be hyper-vigilant, for example, walking down the road. We use our eyes to look out for obstacles or beautiful flowers, but our blind sight is alert for tigers or cars barrelling out of nowhere. This blind sight also monitors objects that are truly there, but moving as expected. Experienced drivers, for example, are able to note potential hazards which may not be doing anything noticeably dangerous at all, such as a mother walking with a toddler or the other cars on the road. Just as our vision operates on two levels, it has been shown that all our other senses operate in a similar way. After all, we use our senses to evaluate the world, and we evaluate the world so that we can survive it!

With all this brain activity going on, no wonder we are quick to accept nearly any statement as fact. Don't underestimate the power of suggestion, even at the most basic level.

A disc jockey on the radio station Jazz FM learned on his show one morning that not only are yawns visually contagious, but that we will yawn even if we hear the sound of yawning. The DJ thought this was fun and to test the theory began making yawning sounds during breaks in his show. I was feeding my six-month-old at the time and I am rather sure her comprehension of language did not include an understanding of experiments and yawning.

She yawned like mad, following the cues coming from the radio. It made feeding her quite difficult and I was very tempted to ring the station up to tell the disc jockey to call his experiment off!

Most people are happy to accept, however, that small children are prone to suggestion. Surely adults are immune, with our more mature mental abilities?

I was recalling this yawning episode not long ago and thinking absently about how our dog yawning can make the baby yawn, and vice versa. After mulling over yawning contagion for about five minutes, I could feel myself needing to yawn! I was very conscious of the relationship between seeing a yawn and being compelled to yawn, but even the idea of yawning made me yawn. Our neurological patterns are clearly very difficult to overthrow.

Psychologist Carl Dunker set up an experiment where the subjects, university students, were asked to make a pendulum. The participants were admitted to a room where a weight attached to a length of cord and a nail were lying on a table. The trick was that there was no hammer to use to put the nail into the wall. Only half of the students were able to solve the problem by using the weight as a hammer.

More recently, other experiments using experienced engineers as subjects have shown that mental blocks are difficult to overcome even in inherently creative exercises. For example, when asked to design a spill-proof cup without a mouthpiece, the engineers found it difficult to eliminate conventional thought patterns, and a good half still incorporated a mouthpiece into their designs.

Our brains are designed to accept conventions and form mental habits quickly. Being told that an object is a pendulum weight prejudices our brain against forming an alternate conception of its identity. Imagine how much more difficult it is for our brains to make leaps outside of accepted conventions with more complicated problems, where the distracting obstacles are more complex than the question 'What can I use as a hammer?'

Surrounding yourself with passive fragments of information and experience is to subsume your innate critical abilities to an external, apparent statement of fact. The more you limit your direct experience of the world, the less you are able to combat the formation of these mental habits. It has nothing to do with intelligence and everything to do with a determined effort to maintain your own presence of mind. Simple changes such as I have suggested can reactivate your critical abilities and put you back in control of your brain, give you a clearer vision of reality, and also help you build respect for your own intelligence and abilities.

Establishing positive thought patterns is not just so that you can walk around with an inane grin on your face. Positive thinking is in fact a way of unleashing your brain power and increasing your alertness. You do not have to have a career to stimulate your brain, you see. You just need to exercise a little self-respect.

Eventually, the ultimate show of respect is to act on your ideas. Writing them down, or pasting together scrapbooks will eventually be a tool for future inspiration leading to activity or deeper, more analytical study.

In this chapter we have looked at the basic skill of suspending judgement by eliminating negative influences. By suspending judgement, your awareness of your surroundings becomes heightened and in turn stimulates your critical abilities. This new-found alertness now opens you up to inspiration, which is in turn the kick in the pants you sometimes need to get you going in a new and interesting direction.

7
Inspiration is discovering the world afresh

By clearing away negative influences you have made yourself receptive to inspiration. Inspiration, the seed that fires the soul, is the spark that will motivate you to get you out of bed, give you more energy than your morning cuppa, and restore your faith in humankind. Being attuned to inspiration and making yourself open to receive it will awaken within you the unlimited possibilities in the world. In this chapter you will start to build a collection of inspiration so that when you are feeling bored or blue you will have tools ready to hand to get you back on a fun and productive track. Over time you will find that having quick access to your own private store of spiritual and intellectual treasures is fundamental to living a good, purposeful life.

Opening yourself to inspiration allows you to enjoy everything in life that is actually free. One housewife explained, 'I am much more appreciative of simple things such as birds singing, the sun shining and the baby smiling'. There is wonder and beauty surrounding us all the time. It is the rare individual who has the opportunity actually to appreciate it every day. Fortunately, gathering sparks of inspiration does not require hard graft or money. All you need is to be a little bit attentive because these gems of experience are fleeting. They can, however, lift you up out of the ordinary. Pam shared one of her own touching moments. 'There is nothing sweeter than your little girl looking up, reaching out her lovely little hand and taking yours while you cross a parking lot.' That one observation turned an everyday trip to the shops into a precious memory.

Inspiration surrounds us, but the best places to look are in fun, wisdom and beauty. My Discovery Journal has themes built around these concepts. However, it is worth thinking about everything in your life, your possessions, and even your friends, as fitting into one or more of these three sources. After all, if you want to live a more inspired life, you need to create the right context for yourself. Although all your great ideas seem to come out of your brain, they really come from interacting with your environment, whether from reading the wisdom of ancient scholars, enjoying a joke or the spontaneous play of your children, or admiring the beauty of natural or artistic creation. Inspiration comes from being alert and attentive to the world around you.

Fun

Everyone needs fun. Research shows that a good belly laugh is good for your health. It increases the intake of oxygen, it works those abdominal muscles (I'll take any help I can get in this department) and relieves stress. Just as a good laugh can lift your spirits when feeling sad, it can help to clear the mind when your thoughts are in chaos. Fun and humour can be found everywhere, not just in jokes.

Writer Maya Angelou has in her art collection a couple of brightly coloured, whimsical statues which she says make her laugh out loud each time she sees them. Our family loves silly stories and poems, especially ones written by family members. We also like to pass time on long car journeys singing silly vaudeville songs like 'You gotta have skin', written in 1955 by Adler and Ross, or 'Singin' in the bathtub', a comedy standard from the 1920s.

What exactly is humour? Most people think of jokes as the only source of humour and believe if they do not tell jokes well, then they are not really very funny. Jokes can be good, but the humour often comes at the expense of someone else. Also, being at home means you have to be sensitive to the presence of your children. I have found that most of the jokes e-mailed to me, for instance, may be funny but are too coarse to risk them being read accidentally by children, or else they are dependent upon sexist or racist themes. Silliness, which is much more family friendly, is rarely allowed in mature company, unless they happen to be your closest friends.

Silliness can be clever. Slapstick does not have to be stupid and it is a form of humour that children can easily appreciate. Silly but clever humour which we like in our house focuses on puns, rhymes and word-play. With small children, physical silliness, like pretending to hit our heads and fall over, always gets a laugh. Small children enjoy pretending to have physical power over adults, so letting them knock you down can be a very entertaining game indeed. Still other families laugh till they cry with belching contests, dressing in each other's clothes, or playing with Mum's cosmetics.

Children are natural sources of fun, but adults can ignore or belittle a child's sense of humour all too easily. I have often, for example, watched parents quizzing their toddlers on the names of objects or animals in picture books. Usually, the child rebels at the persistent demands for correctness, and calls every animal a monkey. 'Don't be silly' the mother reprimands.

Well, why on earth not? Perhaps the child is signalling that he needs to have fun, not be tested. So why not join in? Call the pet dog a monkey, their baby sister a monkey, the tree in the garden a monkey and soon your wriggling toddler will be jumping into this new game with enthusiasm. Toddlers know that everything in the world has specific names. Playing such a game won't confuse them if you change the names of familiar objects. There is nothing like silliness to brighten up a rainy day or to make you laugh out loud; and nothing like a child to come up with a truly silly game.

Humorous books can be a good place to turn to when you need a chuckle, but you can also collect memories of times you laughed until you cried. Try setting up a funny scrapbook of hilarious family stories or photographs, perhaps starting in your Discovery Journal. Over time, you will find the book becoming a valuable part of your family history.

A family humour book can be a great project for older children to start. Get them to interview their relatives for stories about pranks or misadventures. They will love to hear about the mischief the adults got up to over the years. If you have small children, start recording the humorous pronouncements that they make or adventures they get up to. It will make you laugh out loud every time you read it, and the children will enjoy having some of their famous quotes remembered for posterity.

Start paying attention to what makes you laugh, whether it's your pets or a favourite column in the newspaper, and try to incorporate laughter into your life every day.

Wisdom

Most people agree that wisdom can be inspiring, charging one to action or perhaps more prudent behaviour. However, wisdom carries with it a responsibility. When you know better, you must do better, or else bear the guilt of negligence. Therefore, I personally pursue wisdom slowly. Ask only one serious question at a time and take the time to understand the truth, whether you find it by reading biographies of great people, through prayer or study.

The truth will come to you in funny ways. When I was working as a secretary, just starting out on Wall Street, I went out for Chinese food one night. Working 15-hour days plus weekends for months, I was exhausted, stressed-out and discouraged. I constantly asked 'What am I going to do?' The fortune in my cookie was, as seems to be typical these days, more good advice than fortune telling. It read: 'Learn to delegate.'

Heaven opened up for me as I read that. I may not have felt a bolt of lightning strike me, but I did feel a surge of adrenaline, which always seems to happen when I know I am facing the Truth. A fortune cookie said I didn't have to do it all myself and, by gum, I put those words into action the very next day.

You wouldn't think that a secretary asking for help would go down very well. You would be wrong. Within a matter of days I was probably the world's only secretary with two personal assistants reporting only to me.

Fortune cookies are not the most reliable resource, however. For another source of wisdom, autobiographies can be very inspiring. I enjoy stories about pioneers and explorers, and how they overcame hardship and made their visions become reality.

One of my favourite pioneers is the African explorer Henry Morton Stanley, who purportedly said 'Doctor Livingstone, I presume?' when the two men met in the Congo. He also is responsible for the naming of Victoria Falls, among many other landmarks of the Congo. I like this man's story so much I named one of my cats after him.

Stanley was haunted by feelings of inferiority. Half of his autobiography is actually a complicated construction of lies. He was an orphan, but he insisted throughout his life that he had been adopted by a wealthy American family. He continued to make up qualifications for himself, even though his real life as a legitimate explorer was impressive enough. While I don't find Stanley to be any kind of moral role model, he represents to me the idea that anything in life is possible. His adventures also suggest that you cannot foresee some of the most amazing things that will ever happen in your life. Leaping into the unknown is the only way to find out truly what the world contains.

Give some thought to the type of entertainment you naturally seek out, whether it is funny films, romance novels or *Eastenders*. There may be an underlying symbolism or message in these amusements that feeds into your particular need for guidance or inspiration.

In doing this, though, you are not necessarily looking for role models. I regard the search for role models as a separate project and I have set up a wisdom resource in my Discovery Journal in a section called 'Heroes', full of pictures and articles of people I do admire. Either they just dress nicely, or they have challenged the *status quo* and won. They may not all be smart or philosophical, but they remind me of how much control I do indeed have over my world, my clothes, my opinions, my health. They remind me that I do not have to be a victim of social expectations or be manipulated by marketers.

One of my favourite heroes is Polly Matzinger. She is an immunologist with some ground-breaking theories about cancer treatment. She didn't start her career when she was 16, getting good grades in maths or biology. In fact her first job was as a Playboy bunny.

Her research goes against the conventional understanding of how disease and the immune system interact, and she faces an uphill struggle in getting her ideas accepted. I have found a number of lessons in Matzinger's life. I believe she shows, firstly, that success is absolutely not dependent upon education, connections or upbringing. Her theories also suggest that what is written about the world is not necessarily fact so it's always worth looking at the evidence again.

The best message of all for me, though, is that a person can pursue many interests as careers, not just as hobbies, throughout their life without any obvious connection or logic. This means that it is okay to be a banker one year and a housewife another. It is okay to dream of running a business some day, but first wanting to get a degree in education. One talent does not preclude, or have to include, any of my other interests.

Give some thought to whom you admire and how they can inspire you to live a slightly richer, more interesting or thoughtful life.

You can be your own best source of wisdom, too, by using your dreams to improve your emotional and creative life. C Diane Ealy, a behavioural scientist and creative consultant, believes that dreams are composed of your own symbols. They are not images that can simply be looked up in a textbook and applied in a dogmatic fashion to anyone's life. These symbols arrive not only from our own personal experiences in life, but also from our particular cultural as well as universally human experiences.

Ealy recommends keeping a journal that not only records the narrative of your dreams, but also provokes a dialogue between you and a given symbol. In her book, *The Woman's Book of Creativity*, she gives the following exchange with a bumblebee as an example for such a conversation:

Me: Bee, what are you telling me in the dream?
Bee: Busy, busy, busy. You're busy as a bee.
Me: That's really trite.
Bee: Trite but true. You need to slow down.

'You need to slow down.' That is your own brain giving you the advice you need to hear. If you are too busy during the day to listen to yourself while fully conscious, sometimes your brain will have to speak up while you are sleeping!

Asking yourself what various symbols or locations appearing in your dreams represent to you, unburdens the process of looking at your dreams analytically. Instead of determining how mixed up you are, which can be the connotation of using dream analysis in a therapy session, you can listen to your own good advice.

Don't kid yourself. As an adult and as a parent, you have lived long enough to have accumulated quite a lot of wisdom. Why share it only with your children and partner? You could probably benefit from a good lecture too!

Beauty

Women, generally speaking, do not do well in a squalid environment. We need at least one thing of beauty to look at to lift us up out of the daily grind. In an office, it's only women who think to put flowers on their desk, for example. I used to work with a woman who kept a cut crystal water glass on her desk – so much nicer than disposable plastic cups!

In my perhaps limited experience, men may enjoy beauty but they do not seem to need it the same way women do. Most men I have met can happily live in a shabby bachelor pad, saying their hi-fi, television and fridge full of beer are all the furniture they need. Maybe a couple sun-loungers in the living room will make it more comfortable. This is functionality taken to its most awful extreme. A woman rebels at this.

Beauty does not have to be purchased, however. In the commercial environment we live in, we can be fooled into thinking that buying one hundred knick-knacks will beautify our homes; one thousand jewels will make our wardrobe gorgeous. They will not.

The Discovery Journal is a good place to start examining where you see beauty. You can safely shop in your Discovery Journal, cutting up catalogues and home or fashion magazines. Then, when you have some idle time for reflection, you will look at your journal pages and see that you find beauty in colour, texture, nature or shape. Maybe it is the ethnic textiles and beads you love, not the designer dress or *chaise-longue* that uses these elements.

Beauty is not just in objects. It is an inspiration for all the senses. Do not neglect music, the burble of running water, wind in the trees or catching on wind chimes, or even silence. There is beauty in scent and also touch. Buddhists define objects of desire as appealing to the five senses. However, the Dalai Lama, the Tibetan spiritual leader, has counselled in his writings that whether such objects provide happiness or suffering is dependent on behaviour and attitude. In other words, the material world is just as important in living a happy life as is the intellectual or spiritual world, but each element must be pursued in an emotionally balanced way. It is possible to incorporate beauty into every aspect of life; just remember that you do not have to buy beauty to possess it.

It is easy to forget the luxury that our senses afford us, at absolutely no cost. A taxi driver told me a story of a millionaire he had once driven and had never forgotten.

The driver commented that it must be nice to be wealthy. His passenger sighed and said, 'It's true, you know, that money doesn't buy everything. Five years ago I was at a party. My allergies were acting up, so I was sneezing. Well, I sneezed so hard that I damaged the nerves that control my sense of taste and smell. Since then I have lost a lot of happiness. Imagine, we have to eat three times a day, but for me I could be eating a piece of toast or a cake of mud. In my mouth I couldn't tell you the difference. I could eat rotten meat and not know until I was sick. I have seen specialists all over the world looking for a cure and nothing has worked. And the worst of it is, even though I cannot smell a thing, I still get hay fever! I tell you, I would give away everything I own just to have my senses back'.

The taxi driver paused and looked at me in his rear-view mirror.

'That's amazing,' I said.

'This man was so sad,' the driver agreed. 'It makes me count my blessings every time I think of him. What good is money if you can't even enjoy your bread?'

Your senses are the key to appreciating probably the most enduring source of beauty: nature. This is a beauty you can enjoy with your children. Indeed, it is often the case that parents, focused on providing a sound educational base, emphasise physical, social or intellectual pursuits in their relationship with their children, while wholly taking sensory experiences for granted.

When I was about 10 years old, I went for a walk in the woods with my father. I was astonished to find, when I commented on the loveliness of a flower, that he liked flowers too! It had never occurred to me as a child that men appreciated natural beauty. I had only ever before fully shared my wonderment at unusual, sea-smoothed stones or brilliant autumn leaves with my grandmother, who throughout her life has possessed an undying love for the natural world.

Even if you live in the city, it is still possible to foster an appreciation of nature. As educated adults, we know how the seasons affect the growth cycle of plants. Intellectually, it is almost too boring to think about, unless you are a gardener or naturalist at heart already. To move beyond the academic appreciation of natural cycles, try this exercise, recommended by Charlotte Mason, an early twentieth-century campaigner for educational reform. Adopt a tree.

Find a tree, perhaps near your house or on a walk that you enjoy, and make an effort to take a good look at it every week. Study its bark, its leaves, its environment, its inhabitants. Very quickly, your tree will become an old friend, and on your daily or weekly walk you will find yourself looking forward to seeing it again. As you become familiar with its habits and endow it in your mind with character, the effects of the seasons become not only obvious, but fascinating.

I had a tree I knew well at university. It was an oak that at one point had lost a large branch. The scar remaining on the trunk was a heart shape, which endeared me to this tree to the extent that on Valentine's Day one year I made a point of taking its photograph. What I loved most, though, was how my tree could surprise me, even in the dead of winter.

It was the first big snowstorm of the season. Within hours, the snow was several inches deep. The town was completely silent soon after nightfall and around midnight I decided to take my walk. Snow is a transforming element, of course, and I was distracted by the powdery crystals sticking to my eyelashes and covering all the familiar landmarks. The regularity of the snowfall was only disturbed by one house which had lavishly installed heating pipes under its front drive, and the tarmac gleamed a wet black in contrast as the snow continued to pile up all around it.

I reached my heart tree and almost did not notice it. Snow had clung to its crevasses, and its heart-shaped scar had turned into a gently smiling face. I was not a particularly cheery person during my days as a student, but that solitary walk in the snow was a day, or rather a night, when my heart, both in my chest and on my tree, was immeasurably lightened.

When you have small children, walking can sometimes seem like too much effort. That's okay. Nature is never very far away, and what better way to appreciate it than to lie back and just look at it? One dry, clear day in the autumn I wanted to take the baby out to get some air, but couldn't be bothered to put on all our clothes and shoes as a diligent mother should. So, I brought a rug out to the back garden and lay back on the grass and watched the clouds.

I had not watched clouds ever as an adult, just relaxing with my hands tucked under my head. The baby was delighted, as she always is when Mummy is an easy victim, and she happily clambered over my knees and poked my eyes. Later, I shared my cloud-watching discovery with a friend. She thought it was such a great idea she made her kids join her in staring at the sky right after we had finished talking. She added a new twist though. They watched the sky at twilight, and stayed out until the stars shone. Well, you can bet that the very next evening I was out there, stretched out on my back wanting to see the stars come out for myself! It was fantastic, just like she said.

Being outside is a luxury that I was never allowed as a working woman. I could snatch a few minutes to sit in the sun outside my office building while having a coffee, but even that felt like an artificial experience of nature.

At home, try making time spent out of doors a priority in your day, no matter what the weather. On nice days, of course, it is a joy to sunbathe and read a book while the children tear around the garden. If you have a garden, you can also make a point of serving all of the children's meals outside during good weather. If your husband works late, then try at least having a glass of wine together while sitting out. The fresh air will be good for your health and is almost guaranteed to raise your spirits. Eating alfresco will also begin to build happy memories of this time both for you and your children.

Nature is more than simply a source of aesthetic beauty. The natural world is also the inspiration for mathematics and science, which is a kind of cerebral beauty. If you enjoy numbers, logic games or engineering, learning more about mathematical and scientific problems can be as awe-inspiring as a vista from a mountain top. I once heard a mathematician give proof as to why you can't divide by zero. If you remember your maths, the proof went like this:

Take any two different numbers, say 9 and 23. It is taken as true that any number multiplied by zero equals zero, so:

$$9 \times 0 = 23 \times 0$$

If you attempt to divide both sides by zero to cancel them out, you would get:

$$9 = 23$$

which is false. Therefore you cannot divide by zero. *QED.*

I thought this was lovely proof, but when I told my husband about it, he didn't think there was anything nice about it at all. He works with numbers on a daily basis, but he still didn't love the mathematical neatness of my proof. I guess this proves that beauty is in the eye of the beholder. *QED.*

Fun, wisdom and beauty, while sources of inspiration, are emotional and intellectual constructs and it is not enough to access the world only with your mind. The pursuit of inspiration through only mental channels while sheltering yourself from physical exploration of the world can result not only in a false understanding of your environment, but can even lead to the self-destructive tendencies often associated with genius. The artist's sense, however, the ability to see and communicate depth and meaning in the world, is not dependent upon purely intellectual or emotional sensitivity.

Cultivating the artist's sense

Artists have a reputation for binding negative emotions and self-destructive behaviour to their craft. Indeed, many creative people falsely believe that they are at their best when their lives are sliding into a downward spiral. It is not true, however, that self-destruction and art must be co-conspirators in producing quality, compelling work. Negative emotions allowed to develop in an unhealthy way can ultimately undermine not only the person but also their creativity.

Ealy comments that anger in particular can destroy the creative process, no matter how brilliant the original inspiration. 'Logic and reason do not compel us to reveal ourselves through the creative act – feelings do. But rage detours the passage of the initial creation away from other emotions and everything comes out angry . . . . The message, however delivered, harangues rather than stimulates, and our creative products are predictable and boring.'

Negative emotions that are not eventually harnessed in a healthy, productive way are creative dead ends. Fear, grief and anger by themselves block any vision of the future. A person who cannot work through these emotions will be blocked, both in their emotional lives and in their creative efforts.

Negative emotions and unhappy experiences can be inspirational, though. Grief can make you determined to find the good. Fear gets the adrenaline pumping, and your subconscious can suddenly take over, compelling you to do amazing and unpredictable things. Anger can spark the decision to prove to the world your capability and strength.

What artists are actually doing in letting their emotions lead them down destructive paths is searching for extremes of existence. You don't really have to ruin your life in order to stretch your experience of the world. The previous exercises such as the Discovery Journal and adopting a tree are fun, unchallenging ways to begin seeing the world in a new light. The following exercises are meant to develop the artist's sense of the world in an intentional search for inspiration. The goal is to test the limits of your senses, sometimes even to the point of discomfort.

Sight

Humans are very visual creatures. Even though we use our eyes constantly, we can be quite lazy in appreciating the information that can be gathered with our gift of sight. Charlotte Mason developed a memory game you can play with children that is also an exercise in visual composition. You can play it anywhere, but outside, taking in a view of the countryside or a cityscape, is best. Frame your view and study it with attention for a minute or two. Then, close your eyes and picture the scene in your mind. Then describe what you see in your mind's eye to another person. Let them quiz you on details to really test your recall. If you find you did not notice much detail, take another careful look and close your eyes again until you are happy with the completeness of your mental picture.

This exercise involves quite a bit of mental work, but over time and with practice you should find a growing appreciation for the natural composition of the world around you all the time. Furthermore, your ability to recognise beauty, balance and order will be heightened. The skills used in this game are valuable in photography. Try using your powers of detailed observation the next time you have your camera out.

As you become more sensitive to using your gift of sight, it can be used to brighten your mood. Gradually you will find your dependence on artificial composition such as we see in shop windows and in magazines will decrease, helping you overcome the impulse to go shopping whenever you need to soothe cravings for aesthetic beauty. When I become aware that I need a change of scene, rather than hitting the high street, I go for a walk or drive to the seaside to give myself a visual treat. Use your eyes to study the details of your surroundings. Eventually you will be attuned to the details that can inspire joy in your day.

Scent

Scent is recognised as a very primitive sense, with data being processed through the lower-order functions of the brain. As a result, we are generally only aware of our sense of smell when we are responding to it reflexively, such as when we smell something attractive, like food or spices, or something repulsive, such as mildew or rotten meat.

This exercise helps put different smells into context. Pick a room, such as the bathroom or kitchen, or your garden, and smell everything, even things you know will have a harsh scent. Try even smelling the things you are certain have no scent at all. You may be surprised. As you do this, pay attention to any memories, ideas or associations the scents recall.

Small children really enjoy this game and you can discuss with them whether a particular smell is nice or not. It can be fun to find out what certain smells recall for them as well, especially since their senses are generally much sharper compared to an adult's.

It is astonishing what our brains lock away in association to relatively neutral scents such as dog breath, hand lotion, toilet cleaner and bay leaves. Particular herbs, for example, may call to mind sunshine, while a handful of pebbles may make you think of wet feet dipped in a brook. Make notes of your experiment in your Discovery Journal to remind you on lazier days of the evocative power of scent.

Touch

Children take great delight in feeling objects, testing weight, shape, texture and consistency. This delight is stamped out as we grow up, as we are endlessly told not to touch anything that may be more attractive or potentially mucky than an unbreakable plastic toy. When was the last time you played with your food, for example? Can you remember what a fistful of cooked pasta feels like? When was the last time you moulded a pile of shaving foam or did some finger painting? Try suspending your fear of making a mess for one day and join your children in squishing custard between your fingers or coating your arms in mud, letting it dry and then washing it off under a chilly garden hose. The point is to be willing to feel the world again, and to enjoy the variety of sensations your skin is capable of registering.

Your sense of touch is available wherever you have a nerve ending, so don't limit your experiments and awareness merely to your hands. Roll down the windows of your car, or drive with the sun roof open as often as possible and enjoy the sensation of movement, wind rushing over your face and through your hair. If it is cold outside then just turn on the heater. We spend so much time today living in protective, temperature-controlled bubbles we can forget what the elements feel like against our skin.

Do things which you know are harmless but make your skin crawl, like dare yourself to let a spider crawl over your arm or plunge your hand into a perfectly clean toilet or bucket of ice cubes. The adrenaline rush these little experiences can inspire will wake you up and the surprise of the feeling coupled with a complete lack of consequence just might make you laugh out loud.

Opening yourself up to your sense of touch has the effect of placing your consciousness very much in the present. Other senses transport you to other times and places, raising memories and triggering mental dialogues. Touch, however, has an immediacy that makes you alert to what you are doing right now, whether you happen to be rolling out pastry, stretching your muscles or smoothing clean cotton sheets over a mattress. The emotional impact is generally more subtle, and intentionally playing with your sense of touch can, by snapping your attention to the present, help to moderate stress and soothe negative emotions.

Refreshing your catalogue of tactile sensations can also make you more sympathetic to others and to children in particular. Touch is a vehicle for fun as well as pain, after all. Exercising your awareness of the range of sensations that your skin can detect can increase your empathy for children who are only beginning to build their mental catalogue of tactile experiences and have a burning desire to touch, rattle and splash in everything.

Sound

For people with musical training and for the blind it is obvious that the world consists of dense layers of sound. For the rest of us, it can be a new experience to sit outside or by an open window and try to disentangle the dozens of sounds that can be heard at any one time.

Attuning yourself to your sense of hearing demonstrates how complex and busy our surroundings are at any given moment. When we are not listening with attention, our mind is absorbed by only the loudest or most interesting feature of our environment, when in reality dozens of usually unconnected events are unfolding simultaneously. Each sound you can identify raises a question. Where is that car going? It that someone's favourite radio station? Are those birds fighting over territory or mating? Where is that sound of water coming from and is it more water than usual? Why is that child laughing? Will I hear an adult laugh too?

It can be fun to tape background noise as well, such as the children playing loudly in the garden or the noises surrounding supper time. I have a number of audio tapes I made when I was about eight years old. One was of a game of war I played with some of my friends, and it is both startling and amusing to hear our childish voices making the noises of aeroplane engines, a variety of explosions and calls of 'You're dead! Lie down! I shot you!' Another favourite recording was made while I played quietly on my own with the radio in the background. At the time, of course, I was probably absorbed in my game, but listening to it now I am fascinated by the other noises which surrounded me on that particular day, such as the radio and my parents chatting in the background. I have listened to these tapes many times over the years and the layers of sound captured continue to fascinate me.

Your domestic noise can be captivating to relatives who live far away, especially when you have small children. A fun project to do with your children is to record an audio letter instead of writing, for a change, to send to far-away family members. A child's vocal communication to the recipient will stand as a stark contrast to their written expression, which can be stilted and all too brief when they are still just learning to read and write.

Taste

Everyone likes a nice meal, but many people play it safe with tastes. Grasping the opportunity to try something new doesn't just have to mean choosing something exotic. It may mean challenging yourself to not be so practical all the time. For instance, no one needs an ice-cream for lunch, but is there any pride if on your deathbed you know you have held yourself back from such simple frivolity your whole adult life? One housewife I know throws a 'backwards' day on occasion, where meals start with dessert for a change, and supper is served in the morning. Her kids love it, of course.

Try deviating from absolute practicality when grocery shopping as well. Why not try the different varieties of fruit or vegetables available, for instance, and make a point of preparing them for your lunch? You don't have to subject the whole family to these experiments, after all. Just buy enough of an exotic mushroom or fruit for yourself.

Experiment with buying foods direct from the farm, if you don't already. Modern mass-produced and internationally transported produce has lost a lot of its flavour. It seems obvious that people don't find vegetables very palatable if only because they tend to be harvested too early and allowed to ripen on ships and lorries at the expense of taste. From a trip to Greece my most lasting impression was of the astonishing richness of flavours from the fresh local produce. Every meal was a delight, and the best courses were always simple salads. It is possible to buy such full-flavoured food here, but you may have to start visiting farmers' markets. You most certainly won't be able to find such lovely produce at your regular supermarket. Take advantage of opportunities to taste new things. You could be very pleasantly surprised by the experience.

Being open to your environment and suspending judgement will allow you to be available to inspiration. You must respect the world and its infinite possibilities, though, in order to be positively receptive to the experiences life may throw your way. With a proper respect for the possibilities of creation, the ability to harness sources of inspiration can be a powerful tool you will rely upon throughout your life.

Inspiration is not just for developing great ideas, either. Sometimes it can help you get up out of the middle of a really bad day.

Dealing with critical days

When I was a toddler, I had days, so my parents tell me, when it was determined by the Fates that I should bump my head, scrape my knee, hate my lunch, be unable to do any puzzle properly and generally just have a terrible, frustrating day. Dad called these Critical Days. I still have them, though I don't knock my head against the coffee table quite so often.

Critical Days now tend to mean the weather is crummy, my breakfast is burnt, I have flu, and the baby is having her own Critical Day when everything is boring, and the dog doesn't want to be inside or out. I don't want to read any poetry, or meditate on my pesky Discovery Journal, or take a hot bath. No. I want to feel good and sorry for myself.

You might have these days, too. Go ahead and feel sorry for yourself if you want to. Then after about four hours of sulking, it might just get dull. When that moment hits, turn to this section. Inspiration can help.

Fun

If you don't have anything scheduled for the day that might break your mope, you will need to be proactive. Children can be a huge help in lifting spirits because they are often quick to fill with joy and hilarity – just what you need for a Critical Day.

The first thing you might try is avoiding the quiet, reflective activities. In fact, what you need is to be LOUD. Get out the pots and spoons, turn up the radio and whoop and holler with your kids. Noise keeps evil spirits away, superstition has it, and it might just work in chasing away bad moods. This is quite a silly cure, so it is best just done around the house with your kids or husband for company. You don't want to be reminded years later by your neighbour about how funny you were singing and twirling around in the lounge.

Knocking yourself out of the routine can be enormous fun and you don't have to leave your house to do it, either. Try playing with the 'Artist's Sense' games. Because they are purely sensory, they can draw you out of an emotional state for a time and get you focused on the more neutral elements surrounding you.

For a greater sense of fun, do something new and unusual with your kids, such as the 'backwards' day. Extend this play to include wearing clothes backwards, or making up rules like walking in and out of rooms backwards. Another game is to let one child be King or Queen for the day, letting them decide what will be served at meals, or even when meals will be. You may end up eating cake all day, but it doesn't hurt anything to break all the rules for just one day, especially if you need to be cheered up. Invent your own games to play with your children where the day's routine is dramatically different, and have some fun for a change!

Wisdom

Maybe you need a reality check to get you out of your bad mood. Try the old stand-by of calling a friend, preferably a stay-at-home friend. If you can tell her you are having a Critical Day and need to get out of the house, she will probably be most supportive, having been there herself. She might even have some good advice for you.

What do you do if the baby's asleep and your friend is not free to meet up? Try some Random Reading. This is fun to do even when you are not having a bad day. Just pick a book that you have found to be inspirational in the past and open randomly to any page. In my experience, whatever it is you need to read will actually be on the page you opened to, not the one before or after. The theory is that whatever is troubling you is working so powerfully on your subconscious that your mind (or the Universe, if you want) will direct you automatically to the advice you need.

This works with novels as well, though you should give some thought to what you select. I find that books that deal with the human experience, like classics such as Dickens, Shakespeare or even Twain, work best. *Robinson Crusoe* is a particular favourite of mine for this exercise. You need a book that will distil your current condition and reflect it back to you in the form of a fictional scenario. Seeing a common experience from a distance, acted out by others, can sometimes give you insight into how to work through your own troubles.

Prayer and meditation are also useful if you have some quiet time to yourself. I consider prayer and meditation to be two different processes. During prayer I outline my problem in emotional terms – I'm confused, unhappy, impatient, angry or hurt. Then I ask for the quality that will resolve my condition, such as patience, trust, forgiveness, strength or courage. I don't ask for material things because I figure God should know better than I do what it is I need. So don't pray for £1,000 if you have financial problems. Ask for wisdom to see your way through this problem, courage to act on opportunities or strength to stick to a budget. Don't put the responsibility for solving your problem on to God. Rather express faith that the Universe will help you find the way.

I conclude my prayer by giving thanks for something good about my problem, that I have a child to be angry with, or a beautiful house that just happens to come with troublesome builders.

Following this formula, I have found that answers often come back quickly, but I may not understand the message. I know Truth has hit me during this stage because I cannot forget the wording, even if the underlying message seems unclear. My brain thinks up stuff all the time, but these thin voices disappear and I cannot remember even an hour afterwards what crossed my mind. The Truth always hits me like a light switching on, not some gradual dawning, and it is absolutely unforgettable every time.

The best example of this was from a time when I questioned my faith. So I prayed 'Why is baptism such a big deal? What do I get out of it?'

The answer came back quick as a flash: 'With an attitude like that, why did you get married?'

I felt a bolt of electricity had run through my body, anchoring my feet to the floor. My eyes flew wide open. This was God telling me . . . something. But what? That I had a bad attitude? I did not understand this response at all.

When the Truth sounds like something inscrutable, I need meditation. For this, I turn the sentence over in my mind, repeating it endlessly. I have had to meditate sometimes for weeks, while chopping vegetables, making the bed, walking the dog, and even focused meditation with eyes closed in my reading chair. When I finally work it out, I get a feeling that God is hopping from foot to foot, touching his finger excitedly to His nose. I got it! About time, too.

The answer to my question about baptism came after two or three weeks of meditation. Then, one afternoon, as I poured food into the dog bowl on the kitchen worktop, standing just to the right of my cooker, I knew the answer. I asked myself, why did I get married, if not for some personal gain? The truth poured out of my sluggish brain as I watched the dog food pour out of the bag:

'It isn't what you get that matters, it's what you demonstrate by doing it.'

Finally it all made sense. I had been living much of my life as if everything were a point of negotiation that I wanted to win. I had to make the world bend to my demands. I had ignored the fact that my life is an expression of me, and not really a contest at all. I should have been asking, 'What can I demonstrate about my beliefs, feelings and values in this situation?' This was a profound change of view for me and it clarified a lot of conflicts I had faced in my life. Finding the Truth is a phenomenal experience. I hope it happens to you, no matter what your faith.

Here is one final trick to uncovering gems of wisdom. Everyone likes to give good advice. However, the best advice we give to others is probably exactly the advice we should be giving ourselves. So when you are feeling pretty good about life, or think you know why your neighbour or another mother you know has problems, write these pearls of wisdom down in a special notebook. Then when a Critical Day hits, do a little Random Reading of your advice notebook. You will be amazed at how smart you are.

Beauty

If beauty is your chosen cure this may be a good day to get out the luxuries we often hoard but seldom allow ourselves to enjoy. Unpack your good china and crystal while making your lunch and use it! Or, how about having a cup of aromatic tea in your great-grandmother's heirloom china normally kept under lock and key? Why not wear your most expensive perfume or your most precious jewellery? And now that you are all dolled up, let's do a little window shopping, but if you are on a budget then leave your purse at home. Browse – don't buy! – pretty things to get you out of yourself.

This is not a day to be practical. Look for settings that stimulate the senses, not that offer great bargains. My husband, for example, likes to spend his breaks from the office in a nearby Twinings teashop, smelling their wares. He only occasionally buys anything there. This simple pastime helps turn his mind away from work by reminding him of our weekend ritual of afternoon tea, a little window of peace that precedes the children's whirlwind evening routine.

Think specifically of the five senses in your search for objects of desire when window-shopping to dispel a funk. Try visiting a gallery or museum to delight the eyes, rather than just another gift shop. A music or musical instrument shop can entertain your ears, while a fabric shop or children's zoo may tempt your fingers. To find a treat for your nose, visit a cosmetics and perfumery shop or the spice section of the supermarket. For more ideas on different sorts of shops to visit, flick through the business subjects in your telephone directory. You will find listings for resources in your area you may never even knew existed.

The sense of taste is probably best entertained at home if you are on a budget, on a diet or are just trying to kill time. Save the opportunity to luxuriate in tastes for mealtimes! An inexpensive trick of my mother's is, before brewing her morning cup of coffee, sprinkling a bit of ground cinnamon over the dry coffee. Meals can be spruced up in many simple ways by using unusual seasonings, such as grating fresh ginger over fish or into rice while it's boiling. By experimenting with different seasonings, you may be able to avoid abusing chocolate or other sweets during your Critical Days.

In this chapter we have focused on increasing your awareness of your surroundings, first by looking at how different activities can increase the amount of fun, beauty and wisdom in your life, with the goal of deepening the emotional and intellectual tapestry of your daily existence. The next step involved training yourself to be alert to the raw data your senses can collect for you, which lifts you out of your protective bubble of habit and enriches the sensual experience of everyday life. These exercises are basically about pottering in the real world and are the fodder for your own creative power.

Being able to tap into inspiration when you need it is not the cure for an empty life, however. Being able to enjoy clouds and challenging yourself to eat something different for lunch cannot stave off boredom forever. In Chapter 9 we will look at the action of creativity. This is fundamentally the putting together of random scraps of data you have gathered from your environment. This process of synthesis is essentially how you create your own Eureka moments.

I must give you a warning, though. While doing all these exercises in inspiration you may discover that respecting your creative self and opening your eyes to the world will have begun to work an unexpected miracle on your personality.

8
A miracle of transformation

A funny thing happened on my way to becoming a housewife. I began to care.

It didn't happen straight away, though. The first thing I noticed is that suddenly I was a lot more patient. Driving, for example, did not stress me out like it used to. Stuck in traffic? No problem. So I might be five or ten minutes late. Who cares?

At work I felt a desperate need to control the course of my day, and stress dogged my every hour. At home, after spending time encouraging my creativity, panic no longer gripped me when it was clear that I was *not* in control. Indeed, for the first time in my adult life I was able truly to relax.

At work, people driven by risk surrounded me, and the need to protect the ego permeated the whole organisation. Blame for bad decisions passed angrily through departments until someone, somewhere, accepted responsibility. Credit for success was often jealously guarded. My stepmother advised me early on in my career that 'Your colleagues are not your friends. Never be confused about that'. While this helped me to build a network of friends unconnected with my job, it left little room for sympathy or compassion during the hours I was at work.

When I left work, it was a relief to stop worrying about other people's agendas all the time. The walls of suspicion began to fall away. I could finally stop looking over my shoulder to make sure there was not a knife back there, and start looking forward, at whatever I wanted to. As I practised patience, suspicion faded and sympathy began to grow. I observed the details of situations more carefully, but analysed them less, and my clarity of vision, quite incredibly, improved.

My relationship with the world began to come into sharp focus in a very new and remarkable way. I moved away from being concerned only with how circumstances affected me and instead became aware of how I affected, and was a part of, my community, even as a passive member. I always knew, of course, that my existence had an impact, for example, on the environment. I have always recycled for the greater good of society. But I began to appreciate at a much deeper level how my every action, even my mood, could have a large and far-ranging impact on every person with whom I came into contact.

I am not alone in this experience. This theme of moral or spiritual transition after leaving work came up several times in my conversations with housewives:

> 'I am actively trying to expand the spiritual part of my life at the moment. This may of course have happened if I had continued working, but I somehow doubt it. I didn't even know what my neighbours looked like before I stopped working. Now I am an active member of our local community involved in various different projects . . . . I have gained loads from giving up work.'
>
> *Kerry, who helps new mothers moving into the area make friends and get involved in activities*

> 'I'm not so narrowly focused . . . . There are so many things in life that affect you and you have more of an effect on others than you realise. So, I have become more aware of others and their needs, as well as my own.'
>
> *Jennifer, who is taking foreign language classes and enjoys doing craft projects with her children*

> 'I am infinitely more patient with my children as well as with others. I am much more tolerant and have really lost that materialistic attitude that is so prevalent. I live for people rather than things now. I feel much more aware of the need to help others and to teach my children to do so also.'
>
> *Jennifer, who is a volunteer working with autistic children*

I find this final comment fascinating given that Jennifer had dedicated her career to childcare. In fact, she probably wanted to go into this field because she had always felt people, especially little ones, were important. Yet, somehow, the actual work and administration of caring professionally got in the way of caring simply because we are human.

Community spirit and creativity are linked

There is a connection between an increased awareness of how you fit into the world and actively fostering your creative self. The brain function is similar during both creative problem solving and an episode of spiritual awakening. This does not preclude the existence of God or mean that religious experiences are simply biochemical reactions. Rather, it means that our brains are capable in very small bursts of shooting into the eye of infinity. All at once we can see for a moment the complex interrelationships that allow the universe to operate harmoniously. Not only is the brain, in a limited way, capable of such detailed and spontaneous comprehension, but you can actually transport yourself to this highly dynamic mental state by exercising your creative talents regularly.

There are four defined patterns related to the stages of consciousness ranging from fully alert to sleep: *beta*, *alpha*, *theta* and *delta*. *Alpha*, a meditative state, and *theta*, a trance-like state, tend to result in creative thought. With some practice it is quite easy to move from one stage of consciousness to another at will. Indeed, people do this for themselves all the time without knowing the science behind it. How often have you heard people remark that their best thinking occurs in the shower, while weeding the garden or taking a long walk?

People can change their brain waves by just deciding to meditate or go into a trance, which is the same process that occurs when someone who wants a break during the day decides to go for a walk or whatever other activity they find to be mentally refreshing. You determine what your trigger is for creative work. It can be an elaborate ritual of candle lighting, running a bath and playing meditative music. Equally, it can be as simple as sitting in a particular chair or picking up a favourite pen and notebook.

What you move into when you switch into *alpha* mode is what C Diane Ealy calls an 'expanded sense of self'. In *beta* mode, fully awake and alert, your brain focuses on your mundane, daily needs such as eating and putting petrol in the car. The focus regards only yourself and people close to you.

Moving out of *beta*, material boundaries such as time, hunger and fatigue slip well into the background. In a meditative state logic and materiality give way to a new sort of thinking where limitations are abandoned and all possibilities are considered. Faith can be born. Forgiveness can be realised. Compassion can be fostered. And of course, creativity also bubbles forth. If you have been gathering inspiration from your surroundings, your brain has become practised in combining meanings with the raw facts that your senses are gathering. In a flash, during a moment of relaxation, it all comes together and your understanding of your place in the world becomes clear.

Quaker writer Ralph Hetherington describes this experience beautifully. 'A sudden concentration of attention on a rainy August morning. Clusters of bright red berries, some wrinkled, some blemished, others perfect, hanging among green leaves. The experience could not have lasted more than a few seconds, but that was a moment out of time. I was caught up in what I saw, I became a part of it: the berries, the leaves, the raindrops and I, we were all of a piece. A moment of beauty and harmony and meaning. A moment of understanding.'

In this non-logical frame of mind, values also become clear. Values are distinct from morals in that values are what you hold dear to your heart, while morals are a set of social rules. Indeed, morality sometimes has to be set aside to uphold your values. The best example of this is the dilemma faced by many pacifists during the Second World War. The moral concerns of killing another human being had to be set aside by many to uphold the values of freedom and democracy.

Values can be ignored when confronted with logic. At work, quite often the environment requires linear thinking, which makes value-based decisions quite difficult. When your work is dictated from above, by a boss or business plan, you have to justify your existence and your actions in concrete terms. Locked in logic, though, you have blocked out your availability to all possible opportunities. Most people, coming into work, often sit down and write out their to-do list, review their jam-packed schedules, or start reading a pile of demanding phone messages. The day, indeed, your life, is full before you have given yourself a second to think!

Once you leave work, though, it is easier to demonstrate how important family is in your value system. Once you have some freedom from household chores, you can pursue still other values, and exercises like the Discovery Journal can help you uncover them. What you will find is that these values reflect what you want for your community, such as animal welfare, justice or education. Removing money from the top of your list of values opens up a whole world of opportunity to make life better, beginning with your family and gradually reaching out more deeply into your community. All these values are underpinned by compassion, so living your values will cause your sense of community to blossom.

Compassion

The Dalai Lama writes: '. . . genuine compassion is not like pity or a feeling that others are somehow lower than you. Rather, with genuine compassion you view others as more important than yourself'. Compassion is what you experience when you realise that cleaning your house is irrelevant when you see your child or friend in desperate need of loving attention. It is a feeling that compels you to action.

This gentle love, compassion, is not foolish. Yet compassion is optimistic about human potential. As a more balanced understanding of human nature emerged within me, I tolerated cynicism, sarcasm and pointless criticism less. I began to believe that there is no point in drowning in world-weariness. 'Been there, done that' ceased to be funny any more.

Cynicism is a rejection of possibility and opportunity. Cynics cannot see the future. If you cannot see the future, how can you have hope? If you yourself have no hope, you cannot risk offering hope to another human being. Yet it is this sharing of optimism which is at the root of compassion.

Compassion is not a mother thing. Indeed, developing a sense of compassion and acting on it does not happen to everyone who becomes a parent or turns away from the rat race. You must be able to see beyond yourself first.

While compassion looks outward, selfishness only looks within. Being a parent plays an important role for many people in discovering how vulnerable their community is to selfishness. During a meeting on our housing estate, one childless neighbour commented that he didn't want children playing football on the grassy common area because he didn't want to pay to repair the damage.

The sentiment was quickly quashed, as we are lucky to live in a community where neighbours are keen to get along. However, the temptation to feel a bit selfish rather than trusting others to be responsible is an easy trap. Losing faith in our fellow citizens and family members happens all the time. We can all be forgetful in our self-interested pursuit of money or even leisure, and parents are no exception.

How many times have you seen parents snap at children whose play is making a bit of a mess? Who is really at fault? Many times the parent is upset at the mess because they believe it is just creating more work. Their concern about the child's mess is purely selfish. When you become overly concerned about other people's apparently inconsiderate behaviour and insist on taking it personally, you are heading down a very depressing path.

Selfishness and compassion, both, have the unsettling power to ripple across countless lives. Selfishness, for example, can end marriages, affecting lawyers, estate agents, children, friends, relatives and even pets. A single act of compassion, however, is like a light, improving the lives of unknown tens or even thousands of people.

One afternoon during a family outing we were waiting at traffic lights. There was a dishevelled, possibly homeless man sleeping on a bench, his hands propping up the side of his head. It was cold enough to see your breath.

Suddenly, a young man in a flashy 4x4 drove past and beeped his horn at the sleeping man, presumably his idea of a joke. About one minute later, a waitress from a restaurant across the street walked out with a hot meal in a take-away tray for this poor man. My husband and I were quite moved by this scene. In the space of 60 seconds an unfortunate fellow human being had been treated with active disrespect while simultaneously another person was compelled to kindness.

It is turning towards the world, opening yourself to all possibilities that, firstly, makes you aware of your own creative potential and, secondly, causes an appreciation of the potential of us all. This awakening can be quite powerful. Experiencing the power of your creative abilities while gaining respect for this latent power in others at some point causes a sudden welling up of optimism for the future which is uncontainable. It is this joy that drives evangelists to bother complete strangers with news about God. It compels people to sacrifice precious personal free time to help the less fortunate in their communities. It convinces those with no money to start a business, or the illiterate to learn to read.

The desire to act, however, is not enough. We usually want assurance that we are doing the right thing. Surrounded by a cynical society that only measures the fitness of an action in terms of money, our worry will not be dispelled. The only way to move forward is through the confidence that arises from faith.

Faith

Faith can be a religious experience, what many describe as a sense of surrender to God, karma or fate. Faith is also a mix of trust, confidence and wisdom. Once you become adept at harnessing your creativity, it shows that you trust your brain to produce good ideas. While giving these ideas life, turning them into projects or even into money-making ventures, you are demonstrating confidence not just in yourself and your ability to do a job well. You are radiating confidence in the value of your original idea or source of inspiration. Finally, wisdom is knowing right down to your socks the how and the why of your path. Wisdom instructs you when you are deviating from a good purpose. Indeed, it may have been wisdom that irritated your conscience about leaving your children behind while pursuing a career.

It is an unstoppable combination of optimism and determination. You often read amazing stories of people turning their lives around, climbing previously unconquered mountains, or overcoming disabilities and disadvantage. Once you push past the fear of failure or ridicule you experience faith.

Your life is a light to others

Once you find yourself moved by compassion and feel the fire of confidence afforded by faith, you will be motivated to embark on exciting new paths. Your determination will in turn move others to test their own talents, as acting on your creativity will inspire others to action. They may not join you in your particular project, but if you have caused one other person to make good use of their talents, then you are fulfilling your purpose in life. This duty is never done. Even in old age, your interests and love of life will motivate not only those who know you, but also people who may only know of you. If you stay faithful to this path of living life to good purpose, you may even inspire people after you have passed away. The blessing of being a mother is that you can literally create life. The blessing of being human is that by merely living, whether in joy or grief, others can be reminded with gladness of their own gift of life.

The mere existence of my man asleep on the street bench is a call to action. One person, with his own private issues and motivations, was driven to ridicule. Another was moved to kindness. For all of us who saw this exchange, and certainly for me and my husband, this sleeping creation of God punctuated the otherwise routine passing of a Saturday afternoon. As I write this, the sleeping man may have inspired you to pay more attention to how you live your life. What power there is in the merest moment of a life!

You don't have to be trying to achieve sainthood to put your life to good purpose, by the way. Everything you do can potentially improve someone else's life. Likewise, the anonymous work of millions of other people affects the quality of your daily life too. The Dalai Lama notes that comforts such as air-conditioning 'became possible not because of ourselves, but because of many other people's direct or indirect involvement'.

The actual people involved in bringing air-conditioned comfort to our homes and offices may be highly annoying. In fact, they could actively dislike you if they lived next door. Yet, your life is physically better because of the effort they put into their work. Just imagine what impact your simple, everyday efforts could be having right now on society. Indeed, the way your neighbour lives her life is affecting yours this very moment in untold ways. What better reason to be kind to the people you meet? Your kindness may ripple on to countless hundreds of people over the next several days!

Besides making several people just a little happier, these ripples of kindness are also wonderful because you have the power to start them at any moment. Spontaneous generosity does not require money or even hard work. You do not have to sign up with the Samaritans or volunteer for anything. Merely opening a door, waiting patiently if someone in front of you is faltering, letting someone in a rush go ahead of you in line, or saying thank you as if you mean it will all help at least one other person have a better day. The grateful smile you get in response can help boost your mood as well. In a society that values cheap jokes, a sincere smile from a stranger can be priceless.

Having a well-developed sense of compassion and faith, in quite a miraculous way, makes you a stronger person when faced with hardships. Frustrations caused by the outside world become more manageable. Grief and disappointment can be handled in a healthier way, and you will find it easier to ward off the deep-set social disease of pessimism.

The pessimist has neither compassion nor faith. She blames the outside world for her problems and relishes her role as a victim. She will commonly be heard loudly pointing to the negligence of the government, her parents, her doctor or her husband as being the root cause of all her problems. As the victim, she is absolved of all blame. As a victim, you can hide behind the idea of ethics and values, crowing 'It's not fair!' without actually being ethical yourself at all. If you want your children to learn your values, don't point to the outside world for bad examples. Be a good example yourself.

Acting on your values

It is important to know where your values lie because your life is a light to others. As a housewife you have the opportunity to be your family's moral compass. Your husband may have to spend much of his day mired in materiality and linear thinking, with little time for non-logical thought. Families don't run like businesses, governments or schools. They don't need plans and aims and projections. The family should be a mini-community of mutually dependent individuals, each gifted with creative possibilities and bound together by love. This does not mean the family is an amorphous blob. There is structure, but it is not easily summarised in a tidy sociological diagram. Direction comes from values, is fuelled by talent, but ignited by creativity. As the housewife and leader of the family you have the chance to educate your family in the values you esteem, harness the talents of each individual and encourage each to discover their own creative spark. In this you, the housewife, are an inspiration.

Making yourself a role model and living your own life according to your values is harder when working. If you are in an environment where only rational thought is allowed, you cannot see clearly whether your life is following a good path. If you are unable to review your values from time to time you cannot receive guidance from either your heart or from God as to your true vocation. However, once you are at home, you have the opportunity to reflect on whether your life follows your values. Knowing your values in turn gives you purpose. I bet you did not expect that your decision to become a housewife could result in finding your life's purpose!

In reaching this point, however, you have to have gone through the cycle of uncovering your own creativity, respecting it in others, acknowledging your relationship with the world, uncovering your values and, finally, understanding how your unique talents fit in with the needs of society as a whole. This emotional chain will take you first through self-respect, compassion, optimism, faith and finally into a determination to act.

There are no shortcuts. I could have told you to list all your good qualities to help you build self-respect, or to shout certain affirmations at your reflection in the mirror, but happiness with your life is not as simple as being confident in yourself. Discovering yourself as a woman, mother, wife, citizen and person of many talents is not easy. But using the prism of creativity can make the journey more fun.

If you have reached this stage of understanding yourself as a whole person, you will probably now really understand why I do not mind calling myself a housewife. I simply find the label convenient. Just as I do not have to explain how exactly my name is Melissa, I do not have to burden people I have just met with peculiar definitions of my at-home job. At the same time, calling myself a housewife does not prevent me from holding my own in debating politics, medicine or quantum physics. If people are surprised that a housewife is capable of understanding complex ideas then that is their problem. I don't let other people's prejudices be a measure of my capability to understand or even change the world. By the same token, not having a special job title actually gives me the freedom to pursue passionate, part-time interests in whatever field I choose.

Possessing a deep curiosity in the world is the hallmark of a healthy, well-rounded person. It is the housewife, almost exclusively in this day and age, who has the freedom to pursue such eclectic curiosity at a whim.

Using your free time to chase after whatever may capture your imagination leads us to the final stage of creativity, the reality of creation. It is this, the end product that started with inspiration, which makes the title 'housewife' insufficient to describe what it is us housewives do all day.

9
Creation: the determination to act

By leaving work you have not slipped into a black hole. Your experience of being at home will very probably change the course of the rest of your life. Of the many women I surveyed while researching this book, about a quarter have stumbled onto a new interest during their time at home that they hope to turn into a future business or career. Another quarter have rediscovered interests that they delight in pursuing during their free time. Only a small number of women are determined to return to their former jobs because they enjoy it and know they are good at it.

Finding projects for yourself that make it exciting to get out of bed every day is what we have been working towards. What started out as a series of exercises to stimulate your mind will ultimately result in a deeper understanding of your physical and spiritual existence in the world. A split second of inspiration will compel you to action, study, inquiry and involvement. You will be overwhelmed by awareness of the need for change.

Sadly, many moments of inspired thinking are lost, bogged down by details or defused by ridicule from others. In this chapter we look at how to keep the excitement and momentum flowing, enabling you to be a powerful agent of change in spite of discouragement, criticism and setbacks.

Eureka

How is it a housewife has the potential to change the world? For starters, the housewife has the rare opportunity to live life with attention, no longer simply swept along for months and years by the agendas of one or two hundred other individuals bundled together in a business. By the same token, living your life attentively also endows you with a sense of reality, built through mucking in with the daily chores and getting out and experiencing the world and its problems. It is this sense of reality that is the seedbed for progress. The human species has not accomplished, discovered or invented everything. No. Your talents and active participation in society can *potentially* carry the human race forward. And you do not need to have a career to do it. In fact, being at home can for the first time provide you with enough time to use your talents fully.

Spending time looking and waiting for inspiration is vital. There needs to be space in your life's work to be absent-minded, but yet still attentive. Caught up in the drive to work, with discipline and energy, you may inadvertently be too zealous in knocking aside the illogical, the apparently irrelevant. If your life is a seedbed you could, driven by the exacting demands of your career, not only pull up weeds but also the seedlings that in fact are better suited to the soil in your particular allotment. The creative individual, the one who will cause ripples across society, must have the leisure to take a look at her life and see the dislocated details not as irrelevant, but as a hint of what the future may hold.

Having time to have fun is important too, since not all Eureka moments occur during the contemplation of serious problems. Play is a perfect example of seemingly irrelevant activity in fact containing the germ of major progress. Many important developments have come about as a result of playthings being applied in a new and unexpected way. The steam engine, for instance, is not a modern invention. It was first developed as a mechanical toy 2,000 years earlier in ancient Alexandria before it was ever put to practical use. The theory of probability was derived when an avid gambler asked Pascal for advice on a safe way to play dice. Galileo achieved his remarkable theories on planetary orbits when he turned a popular toy, the telescope, toward the sky. So you see, having time to play can for us educated women be an opportunity for ground-breaking discovery.

Pursuing a career and then coming home to do the housework

doesn't make you available to the opportunities for discovery which are latent in play, or even in observing over long periods the significance of even your children's play.

Let us not neglect the need for problems as a source of creative ideas. Having carved out time for yourself, you can start to find solutions to problems, rather than, overwhelmed by your work schedule, merely grumble about them. A child's learning disability becomes an opportunity for you to learn how to help, not just a tragedy to be dealt with by teachers or health workers. Living on a budget is a chance to discover new, no-cost hobbies, rather than meaning your family has a poorer lifestyle. Being upset by homelessness is no longer simply the government's responsibility; it becomes your responsibility, too.

The housewife is her own boss for much more of the day than most other members of society. How she chooses to use this incredible luxury is up to her. She may decide her mission at home is to be thoroughly involved with her child's early education, teaching not only educational subjects but providing a sound moral foundation and a loving, safe home. This is a tremendous gift not just to her family, but to society. What could be better than an active, clear-headed and sensitive citizen? There can be no greater present to the future of human existence. Furthermore, this experience of intimate childcare will provide still more fodder for your potentially rich future, if you choose to value it.

The housewife may instead use her leisure to solve more worldly problems and pursue politics, justice, art, science, medicine, literature, education, technology, sport, finance or charity work. You can, as a housewife, break ground in any of these areas, and best of all you can do it for fun. Or you could watch television. The future is yours.

I hope you set up your Thank You Drawer, collecting evidence of how people have appreciated you in the past. Now that we are looking for how we can change the future, it is time to put a divider in this drawer and start collecting Eurekas. Whenever you have a brilliant idea, whether it is a future business or a fun family project, note it down on a card or scrap of paper and store it in your drawer. As you accumulate good ideas your drawer will become a great tool for those days when you are feeling down or simply bored. Keeping your Thank Yous next to your Eurekas will encourage you to pursue your great ideas, too. If while reading over your Eurekas doubt slips into your mind, quickly grab a Thank You telling you how smart or helpful you and your ideas really are. In this way you can begin to harness your past to project yourself into a new and unknown future.

Being freed of the workplace and its confining use of job titles, the housewife can pursue many personal interests simultaneously and within her own time frame. Don't limit yourself to just the jobs and hobbies you have had in the past. Your experience of the world is broader than you might think. Following are several exercises in creative invention, all of them dependent upon the use of random association. Through these exercises you can begin to see how having a wide experience of the world contributes to innovation, even by you, even in fields where you may never have had any obvious interest before.

Tool invention

Not an engineer? Know nothing about mechanical design? Guess again. This exercise was derived from an experiment carried out by Dr Ronald Finke at Texas A&M University in 1990.

In the table on page 166, three parts (such as wheels, handle, cylinder, and so forth) have been randomly selected and then paired, again randomly, with a functional category (such as scientific instrument, furniture or weapon). Visualise in your mind the three parts and assemble them in various ways until you get something that looks as though it would be functional for your assigned category of tool.

All three parts must be used, and you are allowed to use parts more than once in your design. You can vary the size, position, properties and materials of your parts. You can place the parts inside one another, or they can be hollow or solid, flexible or rigid, entirely as you wish.

You have two minutes to complete the visualisation. Draw your invention on a piece of paper and keep the good ones in your Eureka file.

Parts and object categories for creative invention exercise

Category	*Parts*
Tools and utensils	Handle Flat square Half-sphere
Weapons	Wire Tube Wheels
Scientific instruments	Hook Cylinder Sphere
Furniture	Ring Sphere Tube
Appliances	Cone Sphere Cylinder
Toys and games	Hook Half-sphere Rectangular block

Source: Finke, Ward and Smith, *Creative Cognition: Theory, Research and Applications* (Massachusetts Institute of Technology, 1992)

Under laboratory conditions it was found that nearly half of the trials resulted in practical inventions and 13.6 per cent resulted in truly original designs.

A further refinement of this exercise is to cover up the object category column and mentally synthesise the set of three random parts into something that looks functional without any assumptions on how your invention will be used. Then select an object category at random and try to figure out how your invention could be applied to that category.

Finke found that when people were given an object category only after they had visualised their tool, there was an even greater incidence of innovation, with 25 per cent of the trials resulting in 'creative' or 'highly creative' inventions. This means that apparently pointless mental pottering is more likely to result in true innovation than the more conventional method of defining your problem first and trying to uncover a creative way of solving it.

Finke's experiments also suggest that being asked to design a weapon or piece of furniture when you have never done so before should in fact result in a greater degree of innovation. Indeed, a high level of knowledge in a field can set up creative blocks and result in merely conventional thinking. Thus, an absence of expertise is not a barrier to coming up with revolutionary, ground-breaking ideas. Isn't that exciting?

Metaphor invention

The sort of unguided random association we used to invent tools can also be used to play with language by inventing metaphors. Pick two words at random. You can pick them by using images from your Discovery Journal or Paper Dolls, the first two objects your eyes land on, or two words taken at random from the dictionary. The source makes no difference. Next, put the words together and try to figure out what, if anything, your invented phrase means.

For example, looking around my office my eyes land on a telephone and a chair. From this I have either a telephone chair or a chair telephone. Playing with this phrase I can imagine a chair with a telephone integrated into it. Or maybe it refers to the few seats on an aeroplane with telephone access. Alternatively, it could be a bracket where telephones sit, maybe affixed to a wall.

What is happening in this particular game is that the mind is forced to try applying a new context to two familiar objects or ideas. Imagine an idea contained within a sphere with each surface point representing a different meaning or context. In your brain, ideas actually get filed away with only a few facets attached according to your past experience. For instance, the word 'lion' in your brain may have the contextual facets of 'danger', 'king of the jungle', and 'hunter' labelled. This is why when you see a lion leaping at you, you are able first to recognise it and next to recognise that you are in serious trouble. Lions are quite complex creatures, though. A more complete picture of 'lion' might include the context of a mother lion protecting and raising her young, the long-lived fidelity between mating couples, and so forth. These contextual spheres can only be expanded within your brain with experience or work. Chapter 7 focused on building contextual spheres by broadening your experience of the world, while this game purposefully tries applying completely new meanings to familiar, everyday objects.

This is a great game to play with your children and it can last just a few minutes or half an hour if you like, but it can also be put to use solving real problems. For instance, I have a problem making my bed every day. It is such a low priority, making the beds does not even show up on my weekly housekeeping schedule. What I need is a bed-maker. What on earth could a bed-maker be? Maybe it is a device, or maybe it is a six-year-old looking for pocket money. Making up a phrase and then deciding what it describes can help you to solve conventional problems in non-conventional ways.

Keep in mind that innovation, as we saw with the tool invention game, will not happen every time. Telephone chair is not a very interesting phrase or concept, really, but the more you play at metaphor invention the more you will invent terms that certainly amuse and may even inspire you.

Mad scientist: creating alien life

By now you should be getting pretty good at throwing assumptions out of the window when playing these innovation games. Playing Mad Scientist takes this skill to the extreme and is derived from experiments conducted in 1991 by psychologist Dr Thomas Ward. The version my husband and I play (usually over dinner or lying in bed) involves inventing new life forms from outer space. Rather than imagining first what an alien might look like, we start at a more basic level, questioning what is required for life, such as breathing, mating and eating. The more we discard conventional rules about the foundation of life, the more creative and interesting our creatures become. We broke major creative ground when my husband announced that if he could change all the rules, then he would throw away DNA. Once that happened, our ideas changed about how such creatures mated, challenging assumptions like whether our new animals ran in packs or were solitary, how long they might live and how the young matured.

Try inventing your own new life form, throwing away one at a time accepted assumptions about what sustains life or what animals are supposed to look like. If your creature has two or four legs, for example, think about why you made such an assumption. If they can only breathe in a gas atmosphere, think about what would happen if you made them live in a liquid or even frozen element. Could they survive outside any atmosphere, in the depths of space and free from gravity?

This game is easily adapted to your unique interests. If politics, economics or history fascinates you, then try inventing a new governmental system or civilisation. An interest in art could result in a mental exploration of aesthetics, such as playing with what art might be like in a society where all the people were blind, psychic or had no sense of touch. To get you started, try reading a wonderful story by H G Wells, 'The Country of the Blind', which examines how civilisation is influenced by our dependence on sight. The point is to practise intentionally throwing away the most fundamental rules that we freely allow to structure our lives and education without question. In this way, you can begin to see how the world could be different or even how the experts could be wrong.

The point of these three games is to examine how to achieve truly innovative thought. True innovation is dependent on what is popularly called 'thinking outside the box' which really entails intentionally abandoning rules and conventions of thought. As these games show, this is remarkably easy once you know a few guidelines, but it requires some creative warming-up first. The traditional practice of group brainstorming, for example, does not in fact break through to true innovation very often. However, by playing games based on random association such as Tool or Metaphor Invention, or the creative game of Mad Scientist, you can become more skilled at generating creative ideas. Indeed, you may find yourself coming across Eureka moments with greater and greater frequency.

Such moments of discovery are very exciting, but the real work of creation means bringing your ideas to fruition. It can be done! Don't allow yourself to be deterred by the assumption that you need expertise, training, money or connections to give your ideas life.

What you need to make a difference in the world is to give your brilliant idea respect with a realistic appraisal of whether your inspiration is really worth pursuing.

Examining the potential of your idea

Once you come down from the euphoria of hitting on your brilliant idea, the brain naturally begins to work through the process of delivery. You have visualised the future. Now you need to figure out how to get there. The challenge is to do this without getting discouraged in the process.

You cannot protect yourself from disappointment or difficulty, but there are various techniques, some of which you have practised already, which can revive your confidence when you face a rough patch. Charles Garfield summarises these techniques nicely in his book, *Peak Performers*, with the term 'self management', built on a foundation of confidence, micro/macro attention, and mental rehearsal.

Self-management

Confidence

By fostering your creativity, you will have uncovered a growing sense of self-confidence. Confidence is, very simply, believing that you can accomplish whatever it is you set out to do, almost regardless of the problems you may face. Fortunately, you have practised how to remove negative influences from your life, come up with some strategies for dealing with Critical Days, and set up a Thank You Drawer with reminders of all the people who think you are pretty talented. Use these techniques to keep this important foundation of confidence healthy.

The natural outgrowth of confidence is an ability to adapt your strategy to changing circumstances.

Micro/macro attention

What Garfield calls micro/macro attention means being able to relate small details to the big picture all the time. I love those characters in films who announce 'I'm a big picture guy' when someone tries to point out problems. You will get nowhere if you are only focused on the big picture. This just leads to foolish decision-making and you will find yourself lurching from one crisis to the next without making much progress towards your goal. You have to be able to see the components of the overall project.

Likewise, you will stand still if you can only see details. This can lead to a crisis of confidence, as too much attention to details distorts their relative importance and may cause you to see problems that don't really exist. Anyone who doesn't have enough interesting projects to do can easily get wrapped up in trivial disputes and imaginary problems. Housewives are in no way immune to this behaviour.

A goal for many new housewives is to improve their social network and make new friends. Someone overly concerned with details may look around their house and only see the children's toys scattered everywhere, muddy footprints in the hall and worry that if someone does drop by to visit they'll think you are a slob.

However, the big picture should be that if someone came by for a visit, this is a great opportunity to take a break and relax with a friend. Relating the details of your dirty house to the big picture of wanting to relax may produce the lovely plan of walking together with the children to the playing fields, or sipping something cool in the back garden while you have a long chat. The detail of clutter, in this way, becomes a very small, but in no way irrelevant, detail. Your unhappiness with the cleanliness of your house obviously limited your options in how you chose to entertain your friend, but it was hardly a tragedy.

Also, if someone calls in for a visit while you are determinedly cleaning, you may open the door radiating panic. Your visitor may think nothing of the state of your house; they may feel they have interrupted some work you obviously value. They may not risk visiting again, in case they interrupt your work. You have let the detail of cleaning interfere with the ultimate goal of being comfortable with people dropping by! Perhaps being a congenial host, if this is your motivation, can be solved in ways other than having a sparkly clean house. Being able to evaluate both the big picture and the detail of a situation allows you to solve problems more quickly with fewer fits of panic. Once you set a goal that you believe in, micro/macro attention allows you to deal rationally with setbacks.

A great way to ensure that you are balancing both the big picture and the details is to use mental rehearsal.

Mental rehearsal

Mental rehearsal is a skill that is often associated with athletes, studying a ski jump, for example, in their mind's eye before the moment of competition. However, mental rehearsal is a powerful way to bolster self-confidence and work through potential problems. We discussed using mental rehearsal earlier when you were preparing to give your boss the heart-breaking news that you were leaving him for a fabulous new life unless he agreed to a more flexible work arrangement.

Working through your projects in your mind should be done in two ways. The fun part involves fantasising about what you hope to achieve. This is useful for getting excited about your goal again if you find your enthusiasm ever flagging. The more practical application of mental rehearsal means working through the steps of how you plan to achieve your goal, say, visualising a routine you can fit into your day between looking after the kids and the house. You need to do both so that the details do not kill your inspiration, but also so that your enthusiasm does not cause you to rush out and do or buy silly things on impulse.

Mental rehearsal is basically a private strategy meeting. If you set the goal of working as a freelance journalist, your private meeting may be picking the newspaper you would most like to see publish your by-line, or imagining your response to a telephone call from the Prime Minister's secretary confirming your interview date. So what if you start by writing up school news for the local weekly? This doesn't exclude you from contacting famous people for your stories.

Obviously, real rehearsal, the practice and repetition of necessary skills, must complement mental rehearsal. Visualisation helps, but it's definitely not like the real thing.

Before I ever played golf on a real course, my husband bought me a very realistic computer golf game. After playing this game for about two weeks, and scoring pretty well, I actually thought I could play golf.

Taking my first lesson with a pro was a bit of an eye opener.

Suffice it to say I can play a mean game of computer golf, but on the course we play best ball and I just have a good time hacking away behind the others.

Being a great golf player is not a dream for me. If I ever wanted to learn seriously how to play golf, it would take a lot of practice, on a regular basis, and probably mean working with a pro to determine my weaknesses. However, my ability to play computer golf could contribute to my ultimate success.

Seeking advice

Just as I would have to consult a pro if I wanted to improve my golf game, you will at some point have to seek advice when determining whether your idea is worth pursuing. This can be the greatest deterrent you face in following a dream.

The devil may be in the details, but there is nothing more powerful than someone telling you to give up. Let me just say that 'give up' is not advice. If you have been doing your mental rehearsal to examine your course of action, your idea should have begun to take on a life of its own. You will start to feel, as Albert Einstein did when he hit on his Theory of Relativity, a sort of electricity coursing through your body. The type of advice you need at this point is not whether your idea is good or bad, but how to execute your grand plan.

You will usually be told to give up before you have even tried your idea out. I was pregnant with my first child when I told people I wanted to write a book. You should have heard the laughter that met this revelation of my dream. I was told I would be lucky to even read a book. I was told to give up before I had written my first word.

Not all discouraging advice should be ignored, even if you find it difficult, like I do, to hear criticism. When I seek advice and get a clue that someone may be unsupportive in their comments, I get someone else to be present, like my husband or a friend. They are not so emotionally invested in my project and can evaluate the advice more objectively, highlighting what is often very useful constructive criticism.

Once you begin seeking out advice, you will also unwittingly have begun the search for opportunity.

Luck and opportunity

Is there a connection between opportunity and luck? I don't think so. It isn't lucky people who get all the breaks in life. It's the ones who open themselves up to opportunity by treating themselves and their work with respect.

Max Gunther, in his book *The Luck Factor*, suggests that lucky people tend to be friendly, intuitive, bold and realistic. I think that lucky people are also prepared and have a good basis of discipline. You do not have to be born with these traits. Indeed, in working with your creative self you have been fostering these very characteristics both in yourself and in your family.

Friendliness

Being a friendly person in terms of being lucky goes back to the idea of making yourself available to inspiration and opportunity. Friendliness does not have to mean you are the most popular person in town. It does mean you express an interest in other people, whether it's in a crowded social situation or just one-to-one. If you find it difficult to speak to complete strangers, your creative work can help you through this problem. The best way to draw someone out is to ask them questions about themselves. People especially like to be asked their opinion on things. If they have an interest in, say, a topic you read about in the news, this is the perfect opportunity to ask their opinion on what all the newspapers say. If their experience is relevant to a project you are working on, then ask them for advice. You might find your idea gets its first airing in the world the day you start asking people questions. I know someone who mentioned their 'dot com' idea to the man seated next to them on the aeroplane who happened to be a computer executive. They finished the flight a few hours later $3 million richer.

Having invested time in your own passionate interests will also create a magnetism around you, drawing others to you. You don't have to become buddies with, or even especially like, everyone you meet. I have met many people in passing, on planes or at parties, whom I will never see again. Yet I always learned something fascinating in that brief contact.

If you worry about loneliness as an at-home mother, you may

need to give your attitude towards people some special attention. I have been surprised during my stint at home by how interesting other stay-at-home mums are. I have met women who have strong political convictions and are unafraid to act on them. Others believe deeply in so-called 'alternative lifestyles' ranging from home education to vegetarianism and have dedicated all their energy into making these non-mainstream ideas work for their families. Remember that you do not have to agree with people to find their ideas interesting.

Many women at home whom I've met have developed interests they never knew they had and plan to learn new skills during their time at home. This intellectual rebirth is so powerful, many look forward with great excitement to returning to college and eventually the workforce with their new career plans. I enjoy being with people who can see their futures and are excited. I find their company energising and inspirational, though usually these women are surprised when I tell them how much influence they have in my life.

To carry your ideas to a new level, and to disperse them into the world, you will have to deal with people. Friendliness means you have the ability to relate to people with an open and receptive mind. Fostering within yourself a positive attitude towards all people will enable you to encounter opportunities, advice and encouragement that you cannot get if you only seek to be isolated.

Intuition

Dr Caroline Myss, medical intuitive and author of *Why People Don't Heal and How They Can*, defines intuition as a recognition of the need for change. The common assumption is that intuition defies logic, but I believe that using your intuition depends on trusting your brain to find solutions without your conscious mind getting involved. Intuition is another sense you have been fostering with your creative work, and everyone possesses it. The difference is that lucky people trust their hunches, or at least are intrigued enough to investigate the possibilities suggested by their intuition.

While intuition may be important in getting you to act, examining the feasibility of your ideas, through mental rehearsal and other techniques, is imperative. Einstein's Theory of relativity was inspired by intuition, but it never would have been accepted academically without proper, logical examination. And logic is there. Since intuition is a product of allowing your senses to collect and process data for you unconsciously, examining your idea more carefully will in fact reveal an underlying logic.

We know that our brains are evaluating our environment all the time at a number of different levels. The difference is in whether we are open to receiving the full range of analysis our brains can offer or whether we feel safer with conscious and logical evaluation only.

To test your intuition, start guessing about the immediate future. Start betting on everything and see how often you are right. Try predicting what your child will say first after waking up, how long it will take to clean the bathroom, how many steps there are leading from the bus stop to the library. This is not like playing the lottery, the numbers that come out of the weekly draw can not be intuitively assessed. But your brain is constantly surveying your environment. Put that survey to the test!

Be bold

Breaking new ground, either for yourself or for society generally, is scary stuff. Even the idea of giving up your much-valued career in order to look after your children requires a degree of boldness. So even though you may not consider yourself a particularly courageous person, every time you truly want to do something that goes against convention, you are exercising your bravery.

Lorenzo Ricciardi comments in his book, *African Rainbow,* that before committing himself wholly to his dream of taking a boat across Africa using the river systems, he worried at length about the problems of fuel, financing, political instability, visas and terrain. Then, one day, he remembered a Latin proverb '*audaces fortuna iuvat*', 'fortune favours the brave', and he decided he just had to forge ahead, solving problems as he encountered them.

Paul Theroux writes of an expression he learned during his travels through China in 1994. '*Xia lai!*' or 'Take the plunge!' was used in any conversation about leaping on the capitalist bandwagon or starting up a new business.

Bravery or boldness requires a leap into the darkness. However, there is no need to do so completely blind. The flip side of boldness, after all, is rashness or foolishness. Jumping unprepared, without doing your research or considering the consequences, is not smart. To complement courage, a good dose of realism will keep you in check.

Be realistic

Gunther identifies in lucky people the ability to cut losses and pragmatism, but I see these as two facets of the healthy realist. For the most part, I believe having a positive outlook and finding the best in a situation is the way to get through much of life, but let's get real. Sometimes life stinks. Sometimes it is your fault. Sometimes it is something beyond your control. The healthy realist can foresee potential problems and prepare for them, or at the very least recognise she is in a bad situation before it gets worse.

Lucky people are prepared for difficulties, but unlike pessimists, not deterred by them. Luck does not mean you open the front door and like magic you have got the dream life you've always wanted. It means that in every major undertaking you can either react quickly and evasively when trouble comes your way, or you have not only a plan B, but plans C, D and E tucked away for any emergency. Being realistic is the quality that allows you to develop a disciplined course of action, carrying you towards your goal.

Discipline

Does being prepared contradict the quality of trusting your intuition? I believe the two must balance each other. In fact, I believe the discipline of study must precede the flowering of intuition. How can an inventor come up with a new product if she has no practical experience of the problem her invention will solve? Creators here on Earth don't walk around in a fog or live in an empty room and one day, Poof! a million-pound idea appears in their head. Intuition does not operate in a vacuum. It needs reality, facts, and most of all it needs problems crying out for solutions.

If you have been able to use some of the techniques I have outlined in this book – clearing away negative influences, playing with random association, and deepening your sensual awareness of your surroundings – you have been disciplining yourself and your mind already. As you uncover, or rediscover, your interests you will automatically begin reading, signing up for classes or practising the skills you need to become more accomplished or expert. This in turn will pave the way for further inspiration, but discipline will always have been a foundation for your great ideas.

A classic story of discovery is of how the mathematician Archimedes discovered the principle of volume displacement. Displacement is used to determine the volume of a complicated object, say the human body, by immersing it in a container of water and measuring the change in water level.

Archimedes was given a gold crown to test by his king, Hiero, who was suspicious that the gold had been diluted with silver. Archimedes knew the weight per volume of gold, but the conventional way to measure volume was to shape the metal into a measurable, geometric, form. There was no way Archimedes was going to melt down his king's precious crown and hammer it into a block. How could he solve this problem? He was greatly troubled.

One evening, as Archimedes stepped into his bath, he noticed the level of his bath water rose, as it always did of course, as he immersed his body. He was suddenly struck that by measuring the water that rose above the original level he would have the volume of his own body. Problem solved! Overwhelmed with excitement, he leaped from his bath and ran naked through the city shouting, 'Eureka!'

Humans have been taking baths and immersing things in water, usually to clean them, for untold millennia. Why was Archimedes the one to stumble upon this new use of water?

First, he was prepared by his education. He was thoroughly familiar with the mathematical principles known at the time in assessing mass. Indeed, he is credited with inventing many of the most fundamental rules for measuring volume. He was well grounded in reality. Second, he was presented with a troubling and pressing problem. If the king asks you a question, woe betide you to return saying there is no solution! You must try something, anything! Finally, he was alert to his environment. It is not luck that compelled him to take a bath, to be educated in maths or to be presented with a problem that required his talents. Opportunity for discovery, for truly important changes, is around us all the time. It is simply that only a few people within a population are properly prepared, through education or experience, to recognise the clues lying right before everyone's eyes. Discipline tills the ground of your mind.

Everyone is capable of discipline, and it does not require some unpleasant, punishing regime. The excitement of having a great idea should provide most of your momentum. You should also make sure you are enjoying yourself. As soon as you lose faith in your vision or stop having fun you will give up.

Discipline is really just establishing a habit that will over time take you closer to your goal. Some women, for instance, follow a strict and complicated skin care regime. Whether their goal is beauty or youthfulness, it is so compelling that they have fostered a very strict discipline in their bid to attain it. Other women are motivated to help their children succeed in life and have a discipline of providing stimulating play, group classes and other activities. It doesn't matter what your goal is. If it's important to you and clear in your mind, the discipline will follow quite easily.

Discipline is not simply a demand for perfection. It is a need to do a job right. This shows respect. If, for example, you were involved in a volunteer effort of teaching children in your community how to quilt and the blankets were then to be presented to refugee families with newborn babies, how would it be for those quilts to fall apart at the first washing? It's not just the needy mother who has been let down. The child who made the quilt would be upset, you would be embarrassed, the project would be remembered badly and even the craft of quilting would suffer in someone's eyes as a result. It is not enough for you to give your time, I am afraid, if the beneficiary is truly in need of your help. You will achieve greater satisfaction if you have given to the best of your ability, even if you get nothing but heartfelt thanks in return.

Discipline can be a double-edged sword. The positive side of discipline will result in a sense of pride for a job well done. The dark side is an obsession for perfection. I know many people who chalk up their need to do everything with exactness to a finely honed habit of discipline. The consuming need for perfection everywhere, though, doesn't breed peace of mind. What should be pride turns to gloating (a thought of 'I'm better than you,' often inflicted when the loser didn't even know there was a competition) or annoyance when events do not go precisely according to plan. Discipline allows you to catch your mistakes early on in a project and, as you increase in experience, to anticipate difficulties.

Why should a housewife bother to be careful, methodical or even professional in her conduct? I may be guessing wildly, but I believe all the fears a working woman harbours about giving up her career are tied to all the benefits associated with having a discipline imposed by her profession: pride in a job well done, recognition by others for her intellectual or creative accomplishments, opportunities to become even more skilled, and money as a reward.

There is no reason to abandon discipline or pride during your time at home. Discipline demonstrates respect for your experience, and your experience at home can be very valuable indeed. Every project you take on, even playing with your child, contains an opportunity either to move to a new, enjoyable and creative level or to earn money. An interest in pregnancy or child development can be the springboard for a totally new career as a midwife, health visitor, nursery school teacher or even private tutor. There are businesses started by women who used to be 'just' housewives who consult on helping first-time mothers buy baby equipment or child-proofing. Blooming Marvellous, the maternity and baby-care chain, was started by mothers who were disappointed by the lack of quality products available for new or expectant families. Don't discount the value of your experience as a housewife. Treat it with respect, apply some discipline, and you could have a thriving business on your hands.

Xia lai!

It's time to go for it. You know better than most people what you are capable of, after all. When you are doing something that resonates with your soul, you feel it in your body. The arguments laying out your failure are based on logical, but often blinkered, analysis. Not every fact in the world is known. You can make discoveries yourself, which could affect science, business, sport, or your community, in deep and profound ways. When you are on the right track, you cannot help but try, no matter what anyone else says. Most important of all, if you don't act on your ideas, someone else will.

Change in the world is inevitable. It's who gets to be the agent of that change, that is the lottery. I believe ideas are given to whoever is receptive. If you receive the idea and reject it, someone else will get the chance to act on it. Have a good idea? Respect it, act on it to the best of your ability, and enjoy the reward of your efforts.

Acting on an idea that stretches your talents, taking you beyond your previous experience, is a delight to experience. Testing the validity of your creative self is a wonderful adventure. Every bit of progress you make, every piece of advice received about how to get ahead is like a gem. You are constantly delighted with even the smallest of steps. Your success in such a situation is in no way guaranteed, so every minute gain feels like a triumph.

You should be ready to pursue those people who will help you get your project off the ground and even face criticism and rejection. You have come a long way all by yourself already. Making time in your life to look for inspiration has probably introduced you to many new ideas, people and experiences well outside your previous career-driven existence. This in turn should have helped make you aware of how important you and your family are, not just to your community but to the wider world. This realisation that you and your great ideas can make a real difference, working or not, is a huge confidence booster.

What if you fail? If you felt in your heart that you were doing the right thing, if the infrastructure to help you on your way had fallen into place and then suddenly disappeared, don't despair.

Ilyana Vanzant advises, in *One Day My Soul Just Opened Up*, do not give up. Get ready. Success is your due, just not right now. For whatever reason, the time may not be right for your idea. Maybe you have another lesson to learn. Maybe another change must happen in the universe before the seed of your idea can take root. Go back to your basics, work on your discipline, and get ready for the next opportunity to go for it.

You will, of course, face setbacks or meet people who make it clear that they cannot share your vision. However, when these days strike and your motivation and confidence slip, simply return to the basics of eliminating negativity and encouraging your creative self to re-emerge. Very quickly you should find your spirits and determination rising again with renewed vigour.

At the beginning of this book we worried about what the future would hold by giving up the familiar grind of pursuing a career. You had to take a leap of faith that being at home would be an okay decision for you and your family. Well, compared to that, any creative venture you have in mind should be simple, whether it means organising a local book club, mentoring underprivileged teens, studying for a new career, or even starting a new business.

Working women and ex-colleagues often ask me how I find life as 'just a housewife'. They are amazed at how enthusiastic I am about my new job. Boredom and depression have never seemed so far removed from my life. Indeed, I get tired and cranky whenever I even consider the possibility of returning to my former, hectic, meeting-packed life. Instead, I look forward to a growing list of personal projects, family adventures and even business ideas I hope to pursue over the course of the rest of my time on this earth. I used to map out my life with five-year plans. Now all I can see is an endless opportunity to try anything and everything. Becoming a housewife can truly change your life for the better.

So my advice to you? *Xia lai!*

Epilogue

Big, amazing things do not happen to every woman who leaves work to care for her family. It is not the reason women leave work anyway. The real test of whether coming home was the right thing to do can only be assessed with hindsight. So, I'm sure you are dying to know, are us housewives pleased with our decision to give up work? Here is the real scoop, and not just from the ladies who are thrilled to pieces:

> 'I am very pleased with my decision. Every time my children do something for the first time I am thrilled that I was there to see it. Every time my oldest comes running to give me a cuddle, I am pleased. Every time she comes to me because she has fallen and hurt herself, I am pleased that I am there.' *Lonnie*

> 'I enjoy my new role and find that there really isn't enough time. Maisy is growing so fast and I don't want to miss a single day of it. I have no regrets and am planning for baby number two.' *Sam*

> 'I have been pleased, but it hasn't been totally easy. I do have a brain and there are times when I could climb the walls with boredom. But I have to say it has turned out for the best and I try to think of myself as a full-time mother rather than a housewife.' *Kelly*

> 'It's okay, but I am happy I can stay home with my kids.' *Cristi*

> 'I love being with my daughter, but it can be lonely.' *Emma*

'YES!! I love staying at home. I am able to truly know my children and to be there for them. My stress level is down considerably and my children are so much happier.'

Jennifer B

'I am very happy, although I do often think about what I will do 'after kids' and how I can best prepare for this.'

Harriet

'I do miss work. I miss the stimulation, the challenge, keeping up on current issues. I don't regret it though.'

Dianna

'So far so good . . . . There are good days and bad days.'

Christine

'I am absolutely, positively pleased with the decision. I wouldn't have had it any other way. Even through the financial difficulties, it was the best way to go.' *Lorie*

'Wouldn't change it for the world.' *Alison*

'In general, yes, it was the right thing to do. However, I do miss having my own independence, both being able to go out to work on my own and also financially.' *Louise*

'I have been totally fulfilled and my son makes me happy with my decision every day. It has been hard emotionally, as well, though.' *Sally*

'It has been harder than I thought to cope with boredom and stress. I do miss my friends and job.' *Heather*

'Definitely pleased. I am there for my daughter when she needs me and she gives me so much pleasure. She is growing so quickly, I would have hated to miss any of this time.' *Mary*

'Yes. These have been the best years of my life.'

Jennifer

As you can see, at least trying to be home full time was worth the risk for these women. They all agree that it is not necessarily easy, but your love for your children makes being at home worthwhile. The decision is really yours to make. No matter what you decide to do, however, know that there are a lot of women out there rooting for you.

Further reading

African Rainbow, Lorenzo & Mirella Ricciardi, Ebury Press, 1989
Big Book of Stress Relief Games, Dr Robert Epstein, McGraw-Hill, 2000
Creative Cognition: Theory, Research and Applications, Finke, Ward and Smith (MIT, 1992)
Everything is Negotiable, Gavin Kennedy, Business Books Limited, 1989
Family Man: Fatherhood, Housework and Gender Equity, Scott Coltrane (OUP, 1996)
Four Arguments for the Elimination of Television, Jerry Mander, William Morrow & Company Inc, 1978
Fresh-Air Fiend, Paul Theroux, Hamish Hamilton, 2000
How to Avoid Housework, Paula Jhung, Fireside, 1995
How Children Learn, John Holt, Penguin Books, 1991
The Luck Factor, Max Gunther, Macmillan, 1977
One Day My Soul Just Opened Up, Ilyana Vanzant, Fireside, 1998
Original Homeschooling Series, Charlotte M Mason, Charlotte Mason Research & Supply, 1993
Peak Performers, Charles Garfield, Avon Books, 1991
Phantoms in the Brain, V S Ramachandran, Fourth Estate, 1999
A Quaker Book of Wisdom, Lawrence Smith, Orion, 1998
Quaker Faith & Practice, Quaker Home Service, 1999
Robinson Crusoe, Daniel Defoe, Bantam Classic, 1988
Simple Abundance, Sara Ban Breathnach, Bantam Press, 1995
Staying Home Instead, Christine Davidson, Jossey-Bass Publishers, 1998
Tao Te Ching, Lao Tzu, Kyle Cathie, 2000
Why People Don't Heal and How They Can, Dr Caroline Myss, Bantam, 1998
The Woman's Book of Creativity, C Diane Ealy, Celestial Arts, 2000

Addresses and websites

Addresses

Education Otherwise
PO Box 7420
London N9 9SG

Tel: 0870 7300074
Website: www.education-otherwise.org

National Chlidbirth Trust
Alexandra House
Oldham Terrace
Acton
London W3 6NH

Tel: 0208 992 8637
Website: www.nct-online.org

Women's Aid Federation of England
PO Box 391
Bristol BS99 7WS

National Domestic Abuse Hotline: 08457 023468
Website: www.womensaid.org.uk

Websites

www.babyworld.co.uk
www.ivillage.com
www.parent-link.co.uk
www.women.com

Index